The Girls' Life

Guide to Growing up

COMPILED & EDITED BY KAREN BOKRAM
ALEXIS SINEX
ILLUSTRATED BY DEBBIE PALEN

Volume 1 of 2

16
EasyRead Large

Copyright Page from the Original Book

Published by
Beyond Words Publishing, Inc.
20827 NW Cornell Road, Suite 500
Hillsboro, Oregon 97124
503-531-8700/1-800-284-9673
www.beyondword.com

The information contained in this book is intended to be educational and not for
diagnosis, prescription, or treatment of mental and/or physical health disorders,
whatsoever. This information should not replace competent medical and/or
psychological care. The authors and publisher are in no way liable for any use
or misuse of the information.

ISBN: 1-58270-026-5

Edited by Michelle Roehm
Designed by Andrea L. Boven
Proofread by Laura Carlsmith
Printed in the United States of America
Distributed to the book trade by Publishers Group West

Library of Congress Catalog Card Number: 00-027-192

The corporate mission of Beyond Words Publishing, Inc.: *Inspire to Integrity*

RHYW

TABLE OF CONTENTS

Karen's Page

We at *Girls' Life* always get letters asking for advice. Snail mail, e-mail, phone calls, you name it. While the concerns have changed a lot even since we started the magazine ("How do I know my on-line crush isn't some pervert?" "Could a shooting happen at my school?"), it always amazes me how much most of the problems are the same. ("My BFF dumped me." "This guy won't pay attention to me." "My mom doesn't get me.").

The best part of this job has always been meeting with girls one-on-one and hearing what is going on in their lives. Often, I am asked for some great life lesson or word of advice. I hardly know what to answer. We each go through such a unique process growing up, so how could I ever come up with one universal truth? But after giving it much thought, here goes: Never, ever leave frosted, fruit-filled PopTarts unattended in the toaster. Especially *my* toaster.

Conveniently located under a wooden kitchen cabinet, my toaster loosely interprets the "light" setting as something just shy of nuclear meltdown. I shudder to tell you about the morning I ran upstairs to blow-dry, only to come back down to find my breakfast flambée-ing nicely, flames nearly touching the tinderbox that houses my priceless collection of Smurf glasses (and to think they started out life at just 99 cents, while supplies lasted).

PopTarts, I've decided, could possibly serve as the world's next wonder fuel. While other breakfast foods, like toast and English muffins, merely disintegrate into crumbs, you could have a barbecue over a PopTart.

And you have to admire the tenacity and downright bravado of a burning PopTart. Unplug the toaster and your frosted cherry with red sugar sprinkles will only continue to roast in bold defiance. You cannot tame the beast.

I panicked at first, thinking I'd be burning down a national forest by lunchtime. (I live 300 miles from anything vaguely resembling Smokey the Bear territory, but this is a PopTart!) Then I discovered the ancient Chinese secret of PopTart removal—chopsticks. Grab a pair, gingerly grasp the offending PopTart and in one clean motion fling into sink (spring, summer, fall) or snow pile (winter only, and don't forget to open the kitchen window first). So there you have it. My one great truth—a watched PopTart never burns.

I know some people may feel cheated by this, but fact is, I have advice on a million things—and none at all. Why? Truthfully, for as much advice as someone else can give girls, they often already have the best answers. Sometimes it takes hearing it from a trusted person (or their favorite magazine). Sometimes it takes talking over the problem. But most of the time, we girls just need someone else to say what that little voice in our heads and heart already is telling us to do.

There is no crime in asking for advice. And there is even less crime in asking for help. Girls need to know that they are not alone in this journey. It's my hope that after reading this book, girls will feel confident in dealing with the tough stuff. Girls just need to weigh their options, listen to people who genuinely care about them, and then use their best judgment and do what they believe is right. So maybe that's my best advice. That and to get a toaster oven.

When we first had the idea for *The* Girls' Life *Guide to Growing Up,* I don't think we had a clue what we were getting ourselves into. It all started innocently enough. *Girls' Life* readers would write us and ask for advice on things. Sometimes normal things like guys, family, puberty, friends, school. Sometimes oddball questions like, "Does getting your period stunt your growth?" (No, not unless you smoke your tampons. Oh, just kidding).

Anyway, after six-plus years of doing Girls' Life, we sure had some answers. Why not, we thought, put them all in one place so girls could reference them over and over as the need arose? And with that, a book was born. And by the time we delivered it, it was about twice the size of the one you are holding. Literally.

Our intrepid, patient, wonderful, talented book editor Michelle gave us the bad news. Time to trim. What a buzz kill. We could barely spare a word. After lots of debate and late nights, we got the book down to a meager 300+ pages. What you are holding in your hands is, we think, the best of the best. While we do credit each author in the back of this book, I would like to give a major hearty thanks to those whose talents make *The* Girls' Life *Guide to Growing Up* and *Girls' Life* magazine great.

Here's to my fabulous and foxy regular contributors—writer Roni Cohen-Sandler and senior contributing editor Michelle Silver. Where would Girls' Life be without your wise words?

And I could never thank enough our favorite advice guru, Carol Weston, our own Dear Carol. Be sure to check out her books *Private and Personal, For Girls Only,* and *Girltalk* for more great girl guidance. Many thanks also to Bill and Dave, who bravely answer the question, "Why are guys so clueless?" a hundred different ways. You two are the best.

As they say, behind every great magazine is a super talented team of editors and writers (really, they do say that). For the past seven years, Girls' Life has been lucky enough to have some of the best.

Thanks a million to executive editor Kelly White, who makes every sentence come alive. Thanks to art king Chun Kim, who dazzles us, issue in and issue out, with his amazing design skills. (How do you put up with all of us? Remember, we love you.) Thanks to copy babes Georgia Wilson and Debbie Chaillou, who make sure all our text is, well, English. And thanks to all the awesome editors who have made *Girls' Life* the best mag around—Jennifer Lawrence, Kerstin Czarra, Kristen Kemp, Miki Hicks, Molly Dougherty, and Sarah Cordi.

And thank you, Eric and Jack, for not only having faith in *Girls' Life* when no one else did, but also for never once wondering aloud what the heck we're writing about this issue.

Okay, nobody but my mom must still be reading at this point, but I am saving the best for last. We could never have done this book without Michelle Roehm and all of the great folks at Beyond Words. Thanks, Debbie Palen, for the adorable illustrations.

And, finally, mucho thanks and big kisses to my co-editor on this book, Lucky Sinex—you are up to any challenge. I never could have done this without your talent. Hey Luck, anything you want to add? "Thanks to my mom for inspiration, for being there throughout all the stages—you know?" She knows. Suzi, you rock.

Phew, am I done yet? Almost. Thanks most of all to you, our readers. Not only are you the biggest contributors to this book, but you are the reason we did it in the first place.

You can start reading now.

Letter from Lucky

As recently as a couple of years ago (I'm 17 now), dinner at my house consisted of a few meaningless exchanges of words but mostly just stony silence. The kind of silence that made chewing noises seem annoyingly exaggerated.

Then one night, my mom, in a sincere attempt to have a real conversation with me, asked, "So ... what do girls your age like to do?" I answered in a terse, stubborn tone, "I dunno—go to parties, hang out...." My mom smiled and said, "That's nice!"

But I looked down at my plate, frustrated. All I could think was how much she didn't know and how much I wished she did. There were confusing things in my life. But as much as I wanted my mom to understand, I had no interest in sharing everything with her.

Why? Well, my mom and I were at an awkward stage. It's not that she didn't have good advice. I just felt my life was way more complicated and a lot different than when she was growing up. I had issues with boys and dating, school pressure and grades, peer pressure, and all that stuff. Things I sure wasn't comfortable discussing with my mom, of all people.

No way would she understand how things are now, how much more complicated things are than when she was a girl. She couldn't possibly tune in to the whole popularity thing. Nobody asked boys out in her generation. And she never had to deal with her parents getting a divorce.

I needed someone to talk to, someone who had faced the same stuff and totally got what I was going through. My friends were just as lost as I was. We were facing mixed-up feelings about crushes on boys who didn't know we were alive, friendship fights that seemed like the end of the world, and family situations that made our lives ten times harder.

I remember spending hours with my friends, spread out on the bedroom floor, flipping through pages and pages of *YM, Seventeen,* and *Cosmo.* We hoped we'd find the magic answers to all our questions. Of course, article after article was about sex and men, things that were only funny to us and held absolutely no relevance. I needed help with my dilemmas.

One time, a boy I had a huge crush on told the whole school I was a lousy kisser and not worth dating. I was devastated and certain my whole life was ruined. Worse yet, my friends started talking about it behind my back. I was convinced no boy would ever talk to me again and that I didn't have a friend in the world.

My mom knew from the way I was acting that something was wrong, but pigs would have to grow wings before I'd tell her what was going on. I kept wishing I had someone to turn to for advice, someone outside my little world who could help without being too involved.

So many things are changing—your body, your thoughts, your emotions, your world—and it's normal to feel lost in what seems like a nightmare with no end. But trust me, it gets easier. A book like this, with good advice from girls who know what they're talking about, sure could have helped me. This book is honest—no cutesy, pretend stuff—and gets to the heart of growing up and coping with real life. It doesn't preach and tell you what to do but instead guides you to make informed decisions and to better understand things.

Take it from me, girls, a little extra advice for all your questions—the serious ones and even the silly ones—will help clear up some of the confusion, even when you're positively convinced nothing will ever make sense!

Love Always,

Lucky (Alexis)

The Girls' Life

Guide to Friends

F-R-I-E-N-D-S

How To Spell True-Blue Buds

Who just by listening to your good news makes it seem a million times more exciting? Who makes you feel like rejoining the human race after you've been thoroughly humiliated? If we posed these questions to every girl from Boston to Baja, we'd hear a chorus of "Friends!" So why aren't we taught how to find these majorly important people? True, you know a good bud when you've got one, but it's harder to describe just exactly what makes a friend a friend. So letter by letter, we've spelled out exactly what it is to have a bud who's true-blue.

DOES SHE MAKE YOU FEEL VALUED?

How can you tell if your friend truly likes you? Some girls are naturally affectionate—always throwing arms around shoulders. Others are more comfy showing they care by what they say or do. As Janet, 14, describes, "My best friend isn't the huggy type. Nobody in her family is. But she always makes time to call me, even when she's busy." Waiting for friends, saving seats, and offering to share your very last blue M&M are other ways girls show buds they're important.

With words, however, things sometimes get complicated. Eve, 10, says, "My friends always say sweet things, like how I'm an awesome soccer player and great friend. I love that." But other girls question whether compliments guarantee friendship. "No way," says Megan, 13. "Some girls try to flatter you, and it's not real." Beware of the hyper-complimenter —she may want to use you.

Unlike a user, a true bud values your qualities more than your DVD, pool or hunky big brother. She also lets you know she's lucky to have you as a friend. A real friend makes you feel like a million bucks.

DO YOU RESPECT HER?

It may be tempting to be friends with the girl whose whispered critiques of classmates provoke rounds of giggles from the others (there's one in every school). Maybe the target of their laughter had the "wrong" shoes, a bad-call haircut or a snort for a laugh. Girls say these "victim bashings" happen all the time and without mercy. Nikki, 12, confides, "I know it's not fair, but the girls who live in the smallest houses or can't afford expensive clothes are ignored by the popular girls. It's like they're not good enough."

Some girls are squirming guiltily—it can be hard to resist being one of the popular's chosen few. But when picking friends, it's important to consider whether you respect how she judges and treats others. Picking a potential friend on the basis of wealth (how many bathrooms are in her house?), clothes (how much Calvin is in her closet?) or possessions (where is her cell phone?) may sound ridiculous, but it happens all the time. You've heard it a million times, but we'll say it again: It's what's on the inside that counts.

There's another, more immediate (and potentially harmful) risk in befriending someone who thinks it's her job to cut on everyone: If she does it to others, is your turn coming?

IS SHE INTERESTING?

Image 1.1

Your friend doesn't have to win an electrophysics scholarship or tour the world by junior high, but she needn't be an ignoramus. If she's got nothing but empty space in her attic, exploring together will be pretty boring. You can only discuss the merits of Kate Spade bags for so long.

Having a friend who knows what's going on in the world, who has interests of her own and can appreciate yours, can spark lively debates and provide food for thought. Don't agree on everything? Even better. Hearing other points of view helps you figure out where you stand.

Amanda, 12, says, "My friend and her family are into politics. Even though my parents vote for the other side, I love to have dinner at her house 'cause they have awesome arguments." Despite not sharing her friend's interest, Suze, 11, also learns from her friend. "Katie's been into riding her whole life," she says. "I've never been on a horse, and I don't plan to either. But it's fun hearing about the competitions, her biggest rivals, and all the places she goes." Whether your friend is an environmental crusader, a collector of awesome stamps, a master of lanyards, or an authority on gerbils, she knows stuff you don't. She brings different ideas and experiences to the friendship.

Also, you don't have to be identical twins. A good bud is comfy with each of you being your own person. Unlike some friends who are all smiles as long as you're doing things their way, your true bud doesn't require you to hate rap, like French pastries or try smoking. A good friend understands that each of you has to make her own personal decisions. And she knows that having your own thoughts, interests and even mannerisms keeps your brains—and the friend-ship—much more exciting. (Image 1.1)

IS SHE EXCEPTIONALLY TRUSTWORTHY?

There's the obvious sort of trust. You wouldn't want a friend to double-cross you, rat on you or spread rumors about you. But we're also talking about the more subtle kind of trust which, when earned, makes a friend amazing.

Dear Carol: I have a friend who is bossy, demand-ing, pushy, and powerful. I like her, but we fight a lot, and it seems like I hate her. How do I say bye for good?—SINKING FRIENDSHIP

Dear Sinking Friendship: It's good to recognize which friendships make you feel good and which drag you down. If you two can't (or don't want to) work things out, give yourselves some breathing room. Don't dump her in a dramatic way, or diss her left and right. Try joining activities that she's not in, and start calling and making plans with others.

If you can't count on your good friend to tell you when your zipper's open or your bra strap's making an appearance, who can you trust? When the subject's more personal, it gets even trickier. Ali, 13, confesses that at first it wasn't easy to hear what her best friend had to say. "She basically told me I was too flirty with guys and was getting a bad rep. I was ticked off at first! But later I realized what courage it must have taken for her to tell me. It's not like she wanted me to feel bad. She knew I'd be better off knowing."

On the other hand, there's a fine line here: *How* your friend tells you is part of the trust. Melanie, 13, found out the hard way. "My friend told me I had a huge zit while we were standing in the middle of the lunch line," she says. "She said it loudly, too. And it wasn't like I didn't know!" Afterward, Melanie wondered, "How could she have said it in front of everyone? It was so mean!"

When friends feel close enough to mention the unmentionable, saving you from embarrassment, that's trust. When they humiliate you, that's betrayal.

IS SHE A NOTCH ABOVE?

We'd rather mention these qualities last because they're bonuses—but then we'd be spelling FRIEDSN. First, if your friend has a sense of humor, cool. You know those moments when you're on the verge of tears or losing it? Then you catch your bud's smirk, and the next thing you know you're both cracking up.

While laughter is great medicine, not all ailments can be cured by a session of giggles. That's when you need a friend who's "a notch above"—willing to go above and beyond the call of duty. Lots of friends can be sweet, kind, and thoughtful. But it's the rare friend who will do these things even when it's totally not convenient for her.

For example, Tracy, 14, says, "When a rumor was going all around school about me, my friend did not ignore it. She marched right up to the kids who started it and blasted 'em. She couldn't have cared less if they got mad."

IS SHE DEPENDABLE?

Your friend might be reliable in showing up when she says she will, or doing her share of a group project. Then again, Holly, 12, says not all good friends can even pull this off. "My friend," she says, "is a total flake. But she's got lots of good qualities too. So I've learned not to let her borrow my best stuff." Living with friends who are late or forgetful isn't the worst thing. If you can stand it, great. But another kind of dependability test often makes or breaks a friendship: Is your friend loyal?

If, for example, your group decides this week you're the one they'll be mad at, what will your friend do? Will she go along, saying, "Sorry, no choice!"? Or will she stick by you? If you've been left out of weekend plans, accidentally or otherwise, will she remind others that you exist? Tara, 12, has a good example: "On a field trip, we were split into groups, and I was put on a bus all by myself. When Julie saw what had happened, she got right off that bus and went with me."

Let's face it, the social scene can be nerve-wracking. Having a friend's loyalty is like carrying around a good-luck charm.

IS SHE A GIRL OF SUBSTANCE?

Not every friend can—or should be expected to—fulfill all your needs. But a great friend is someone you can turn to when something big is on your mind. We're not talking gym socks here—your gym teacher's dorky knee-highs can be hashed with anybody (except the gym teacher). But some things are too important—saved strictly for confidantes.

Aimee, 12, says, "Last year when my grandmother died, I was confused and upset. There was only one friend I could talk to. I definitely felt lucky to have her." A friend of substance doesn't ignore you when something bad happens in your life.

You want to share your most personal thoughts with a friend who's comfortable with feelings. She should be a good listener, understand the seriousness of what you're telling her, and be able to imagine herself in your shoes. When you tell a girl of substance something that matters, she's there for you.

While not all friends need to have every quality, really good friends should. And double-check yourself every once in a while. That's what F-R-I-E-N-D-S are for.

25 Reasons Why Girlfriends Rock

1. She can lift your spirits when you're in the dumps.

2. She's always on the lookout for the perfect guy.

3. She'll guard the bathroom door.

4. She'll pick up your homework when you're sick.

5. She buys you the silliest souvenirs when she's on vacation.

6. She keeps a lookout for your crush.

7. She makes time after school to help you study.

8. She knows all the dirt from your past ... and keeps it to herself.

9. She never laughs when you trip in public.

10. She never tells you to shut up when you are crooning your favorite tunes, even though your voice is bad.

11. After reading her horoscope, she checks out yours and clues you in.

12. She takes your back when you slip in late for class.

13. She makes up the sweetest white lies.

14. She thinks you look great without makeup.

15. She lets you moan about your problems ... for hours.

16. She brings out the silly side in you.

17. She always has good advice to give you.

18. She shares your embarrassing moments.

19. She lends you a shoulder to cry on.

20. She gets along with your parents.

21. She lets you borrow her clothes on a weekly basis.

22. She lends you $5 when you forget your lunch money.

23. She makes you number one on her speed dial.

24. She knows what you are thinking before you even say it.

25. She thinks you rock and lets you know it.

—KRISTEL BOE, 15

Quiz:

Best Bud Challenge

"We're like two peas in a pod," you claim. "I know her better than she knows herself." But do you really know your BFF as well as you think? There's one way to find out. Grab a pen and your best bud. Take turns answering the following questions. Give each other a point for every right answer, and then check your score to see if you two really are of the same pod.

WOULD SHE OR WOULDN'T SHE?

Write true or false in the blanks as to how you think your BFF would behave.

If the school bully was being nasty and calling a second grader "Shrimp," your BFF would be the first to stand up for her. _____

She'd be honest and tell you if your mini was too mini before you showed your undies to the entire middle school. _____

If she found a twenty-dollar bill on the sidewalk, she'd stuff it in her pocket and swear she had dropped it. _____

She'd lie to your parents and hers if it meant you wouldn't be grounded for a month. _____

The dog has definitely eaten her homework more than once. _____

If your mom asked for help washing the dishes after you and your BFF cooked dinner, she'd be out the door before you could blink an eye. _____

If you two were crushing over the same guy, she'd be happy for you if he called. _____

PICK HER FAVORITES

Circle the item in each category that your BFF likes the most.

Clothes: embroidered jeans, Adidas sweats, a black tube top, Gap cargos, anything clean

Shoes: flip flops, Doc Martens, Nikes, platform knee-hi boots, red sling back wedges

Food: veggie burger, pizza, burrito, sushi, peanut butter and jelly sandwich

CD: Fiona Apple, Mariah Carey, LeAnne Rimes, BSB, Busta Rhymes

Accessory: Yankees hat, cat-eye sunglasses, a shrug, Kate Spade bag, Hello Kitty book-bag

Subject: American history, English, photography, chemistry, lunch

Cause: PETA, Greenpeace, Young Republicans, Habitat for Humanity, herself

HER DREAMS

Circle the letter of the option that best fits your friend.

Twenty years from now, you'd most likely hear her say...
a) "I plan to open a seventh homeless shelter."
b) "I accept my nomination to be President of the U.S."
c) "I want to thank the Academy."
d) "Would you like fries with that?"

She'd choose to live:
a) in the mountains of Colorado
b) in New York City
c) in a country you need an atlas to find
d) exactly where she is

Her first car will be:
a) a Jeep Wrangler

b) a BMW convertible
c) an oversized pick-up
d) a Cannondale

If she could redo her bedroom, she would definitely include:
a) a four poster canopy, lots of lacey pillows, and frilly sheets
b) a futon, lava lamp, and her Phish CDs
c) a blow-up arm chair and wall-to-wall BSB posters
d) a walk-in closet with a computerized outfit selection system

Her idea of a perfect night is:
a) hanging with a group of guys and girls at a party complete with a DJ and dance floor
b) renting *Now and Then*—just the two of you
c) packing a dinner picnic and heading for a sunset hike with a small group
d) spending the evening with her boyfriend at a major league baseball game

Her dream guy will:
a) hike mountains, save whales, recycle
b) drive an Audi, have a gold card, invest wisely
c) hop on his Harley, wear leather, ride on the wild side
d) call back

She'll name her first daughter:

a) after her mom
b) after her favorite literary heroine
c) after you
d) after she gets back from the business trip she just couldn't miss

IT COULD HAPPEN...

Circle the appropriate celebs for the following questions.

If she could trade places with one of the following, she'd choose:
Hillary Clinton, Oprah Winfrey, Cindy Crawford, Britney Spears

Her dream date is:
Justin Timberlake, Brad Pitt, Chris O'Donnell, Derek Jeter

She would most like to raid the closet of:
Marilyn Manson, the Olsen twins, Sara Michelle Gellar, Jennifer Aniston

If she could switch her mom with a TV mom for a week it would be:
Roseanne, Annie Camden, Marge Simpson, Gail Leary

LOVES AND HATES

Fill in the following blanks.

Her favorite TV show of all time is _____.

She is most likely to spend her allowance on _____.

Her biggest pet peeve is _____.

Her dream vacation is to visit _____.

She'd most like to meet _____.

The beauty product she can't live without is _____.

The quality she loves about you is _____.

IN A NUTSHELL

Circle one description in each line that best fits your BFF.

1. info seeker/info giver
2. life of the party/couch potato
3. secret keeper/secret blabber
4. fashion diva/fashion disaster

5. it's always "on her"/splits tax down the middle
6. always early/"Oh boy, look at the time."
7. class clown/classy
8. adventurous/adventure-less

ADD IT UP

Give each other one point for each correct answer, add up the total, and locate your score.

31-40 Siamese Twins

You two aren't just of the same pod. You're practically the same pea. It's awesome that you've found her; you're truest of buds. Knowing each other so well means you can really help each other in times of need and social planning. Instead of guessing what's best for each other, you rely on strong vibes. Still, don't forget there are lots of other great girls out there, so don't tune yourselves out completely to the world.

21-30 Closest of Companions

Just because you're not attached at the hip doesn't mean you're not the best of friends. You're obviously in sync with each other and enjoy talking about stuff that's important to you. You may be happiest exactly where you are in your friendship. If so, enjoy. If you aspire to know more about each other, find out—that's what having friends is for.

11-20 Room for Improvement

You might want to clue in a bit. But that doesn't mean you have to trash the friendship. If you like and trust each other, make more one-on-one time. Go for a hike, hang in your backyard, or just crash on the couch and chat. You don't have to force bonding by spilling your guts, but try to open up. Share some of your thoughts, goals and experiences. If you're having trouble, use this quiz to get started.

1-10 Missing the Boat

Yikes! Did you take this quiz with a stranger? Put simply, friendship takes effort. Try following the advice in "Room for Improvement" (above). When listening, pay close attention, ask questions and make an effort to truly understand her. Be sure she's doing the same for you. You may have to remind each other, but, hey, the friendship can only grow. If it doesn't, you may have to say adios and find new friends who are willing to put forth the effort it takes to make a friendship grow. (Image 3.1)

Image 3.1

SINGIN' THE U-HAUL BLUES

How To Deal When Your Best Bud Moves

Is your best bud moving? It's sad, I know. Here are some tips on dealing with it, staying close, and, gulp, finding new friends. (Image 3.2)

Image 3.2

Getting the news. When your BFF tells you the sad news, don't start mourning right away. More than likely, she feels as bad as you do. Be supportive and take advantage of the time you have left. Spend your last weeks together having fun, not crying over the move.

The big day. The moving trucks are loaded, and you and your BFF are sitting on her porch. You haven't said much—you want your good-bye to be short, sweet and sincere. Finding the right words is the hardest part. There is no perfect phrase. Just let her know you'll miss her, and that you'll e-mail and call lots. Let her know she'll always be important to you even though she may be ten states away.

Hitting the new school year ... without her. You meet your friends at the normal spot to catch up on gossip. But something's not right. You sit solo on the bus while your other friends have someone to sit with. It's obvious what's missing here. But now that school is going again, you can meet a world of new people!

Where to begin? Start by being the first person to say "hi" to the new kids at your school who left their BFFs behind. Be polite, tell the new girl about yourself and ask about her. Just make sure every other word out of your mouth is not about how great your old BFF is.

Make new friends and keep the old. You're back on your feet and feeling good. You have new friends and things are going great. But don't get so caught up in your new social whirl that you forget your old friend. E-mail is a totally cheap, cool way to stay in touch. When you write, tell your old BFF what's up with you and everyone she knew. And call, if your parents say it is okay (long distance costs money, ya know). Send cute postcards of places you two hung out in your town. Go down to the beach you two used to hang out at and send her some sand, or pick a leaf from the tree you two used to climb. Little reminders mean a lot.

—APRIL A. MAAS, 11

Peace on Planet Friendship

They're your two closest friends in the world—so why do they insist on disliking one another? Maybe they won't give each other the time of day; or worse, they bicker and talk behind each other's back. It makes no sense. You adore them *both.*

By mathematical standards, shouldn't they get along? If A likes B and A likes C, then B and C should like each other. Unfortunately, relationships can defy logic—mathematical theory just does not apply to anything as finicky as friendship.

Take Jennifer, 12. She loves hanging out with Debbie because the girl keeps her in side-splitting laughter. "You should see Deb's Britney Spears impression," Jennifer says. Jennifer's new friend, Meg from ballet school, is a class clown who will also do anything for a laugh, including pirouetting herself straight into the nearest wall. "It was obvious Deb and Meg would be crazy about each other," says Jennifer. "I couldn't wait to introduce them."

They all agreed to meet at a park one afternoon, go skateboarding and hang out for a while. Unfortunately, things didn't go as well as Jennifer predicted.

"I had been telling them they would love each other because they were both so funny," Jennifer says. "They couldn't wait to meet. But when the three of us got together, they just didn't get each other's sense of humor. When one made a joke, the other sat there, and I was the only one laughing." Jennifer didn't laugh long. The afternoon was cut short when Meg abruptly said she had to get home for dinner—at like 3:00. The rest of the day, Debbie talked about how obnoxious Meg was. Jennifer never got the two together again and can barely mention one of their names to the other without getting an eye roll.

The sad truth is that this happens all the time. One friend tries to set up two friends who she feels will be a natural fit. Only the fit is about as natural as cramming a tape cassette into a CD player. It's a bummer when your hopes for a fun-loving trio are dashed. What really stinks, though, is when both girls clearly disapprove of your friendship with the other. As the friend in the middle, you get pulled in both directions, defending yourself and apologizing after incidentally mentioning to one friend that the other just won the talent show at the rec center. ("Hello? Do I look like I care?")

It may be sheer jealousy—two friends vying for your attention, intent on disliking "the enemy" who steals too much of your time. Whatever the case, you can't

Image 4.1

force people to like each other. But you can arrange things so you don't feel guilty for being
friends with both of them. After all, it's not your
fault your friends dislike (read: can't stand) each
other. Here's our six-step program for dealing with
dueling buds.

STEP 1: Face facts. If your buds meet, don't hit it off, and choose not to hang out together, that's their call. There's nothing you can do about it, so why try? Just because you adore someone doesn't mean your bud has to.

Often, friends are drawn to each other because they appreciate each other's different qualities and personality traits. When you mix two buds who are alike—same outlook, humor, smarts—they sometimes clash. Whatever the reason, respect your friends' decisions to steer clear of each other. Pushing them together could make them more intent on disliking each other and resentful of you for not understanding. So, yes, you can feel bummed the threesome isn't happening, but don't take your disappointment out on them. (Image 4.1)

STEP 2: Find out the real deal. It's one thing if your friends choose not to acknowledge each other. It's quite another if you feel shunned for spending time with either of them. If they constantly make negative remarks about the other, find out what's causing the hostility. Don't guess. Ask.

• Talk to each friend separately. Don't arrange a meeting for all of you to sit around and discuss the problem. They're likely to clam up and resent you for forcing them into an awkward situation.

- Don't accuse ("You obviously hate her!") or demand ("You'd better be nicer to her!"). This only makes people defensive.

- Ask straight out what the deal is: "I can see you dislike Meg, but why do you get mad when I bring up her name?" Let her talk without interruption.

STEP 3: Listen, and decide for yourself. Often, there's no good reason for one friend disliking another. Your bud just doesn't get good vibes, end of story. But on occasion, a bud will have a valid point as to why she thinks your other friend is bad news. She may believe this new bud uses you, lies to you, or is a bad influence. Hear her out. It's worth considering that your friend *may* have a good point. Then decide for yourself whether there might be an inkling of truth in what she says.

STEP 4: Dish out a few kind words. If this is not about a friend being territorial or protective, and she has no valid reason for disliking the other friend, face it, it may boil down to jealousy. She may be upset because you took your other friend to a concert, instead of her. Or you put your sleeping bag next to your other friend at the sleepover. If so, your friend may need reassurance that you still value her as much as ever. Sure, it's obvious to you, but don't assume it is for her. This is especially true when the angry one is an old friend feeling threatened by a new one.

Try a little empathy:

- You don't have to mention that you suspect there is jealousy. It would probably just make your bud feel foolish.

- Try, "I just want you to know that I love hanging out with you."

- Plan fun things for the two of you.

- Be sensitive. Is it really necessary to talk about how fantastic the other friend is—or even mention her name?

STEP 5: Set boundaries. It's good to keep your buds' feelings in mind, but you also have to stand up for yourself if you feel uncomfortable. You have the right to be friends with whomever you wish—without getting flack from any other friends. Fine—your buds want nothing to do with each other. But you don't have to listen to them tear into each other. If a bud makes jokes at the other's expense, spews nasty comments, or tries to convince you how horrible the other is, you need to set limits:

- Say, "It's okay that you don't want to be friends with Debbie, but it hurts my feelings when you make fun of her."

- If she continues to diss your bud even after you've asked her not to, you might have to take it a step further: "It really bothers me when you say nasty things about Meg. Let's change the subject." (Image 4.2)

Image 4.2

STEP 6: Keep a little faith. Unfortunately, chances are your two buds will never like each other. But you never know—they may come to tolerate each other if you leave them alone. If they bump into each other enough (especially when you're not around), they may get to talking and realize they kinda, sorta like each other. If you're tempted to yell, "Yahoo!" and plan an overnight for the three of you, don't. If they're to be friends, it has to evolve naturally, over time. Any sign of pushing from you will send them running in opposite directions again. So stay cool!

When things go a little too well: Maybe your buds will start to see in each other what you see in them. They may actually enjoy time together when they don't feel they're competing for your affection. They might even hang out with each other, share private jokes, or create their own cryptic messages. Hey! Are you being excluded? You wanted them to get along, right? But you're not so sure anymore. It's easy to feel insecure when two friends who couldn't stand each other become friends outside your domain. Let them. If you accuse them of leaving you out, you're not only going to seem jealous, you'll be a hypocrite. You assured them there was room for both of them in your life. So take your own advice and enjoy the fact you have such fantastic friends.

I Just Got Dumped!

It's something for The X-Files. For months you're totally in with a group—passing notes, making sleepover plans, and sharing lockers. The whole thing. Then one day it happens. The very girls you thought were your best friends in the entire world suddenly let you know, subtly or otherwise, that you are now out. Way out. Somehow, it doesn't matter how long you've been friends, or how much fun you've all shared in the past. There's a saying for times like this: "Into each life, a little rain must fall." And baby, it's pouring.

Welcome to the darkest, loneliest hours girls have to face. We cannot tell a lie—this is one of the most unexplainable, mean-spirited phenomena that happens to girls. And it does happen—all the time. No matter how popular you are, sooner or later the winds shift, and it's your turn to be isolated, gossiped about, and completely shunned. Thankfully, it usually only lasts a few days, often just one.

Ask older girls about it, and many will tell you about the time their so-called friends ganged up on them. They'll tell you how it started, what it felt like and how relieved they were when it finally blew over. Why do girls do this to each other? What if it happens to you? We can only hope it never will. But if it does, here is how to ride out your social storm.

First, we'll tackle the "why." The simple version goes like this: You do or say something that offends one friend. Maybe you tell Jill you think Lisa's new hairstyle is "so last year"—and it is—"but don't tell her I said so." Before you know it, Lisa is furious you're talking about her—and her hair!—behind her back. Or you admit to another bud you got a note from the guy she likes—and she goes ballistic. Or you say something as trivial as, "Ew, gross," when one friend unwraps her tuna sandwich at lunch. Whatever you did, for whatever reason, you've ticked someone off. And she's not planning to let it go.

Ideally, your friend would pull you aside and say, "Listen, you hurt my feelings. Can we talk about it?" Some girls have friends mature enough to actually handle it this way. But many girls seem to think the best tactic is to strike out and hurt you back. What better way than to get all your friends mad at you? All it takes is a little manipulating on a girl's part. She goes to each friend and informs them about the horrible thing you did, blowing it way out of proportion. Then, she tells them what a jerk you are and how anyone who would associate with you is obviously a jerk too. Next thing you know, you're under group attack.

Let's face it, no one wants to be an outcast. So even if the others feel badly for you, there's a good chance they won't risk defending you. (Note: This is not a "girl thing." Many guys also aren't willing to defend another kid if they think they might get shut out of the group.)

Some of you know the next scene well. You're sitting alone during lunch. Your friends are whispering to one another—about you, no doubt. Or they're passing notes to each other and laughing. When you try to talk to them, walk near them, or smile, they turn away like you're the villain who cursed their kingdom.

WHAT DO I DO?

We know what you'd like to do: go up to the other girls and scream, "Knock it off!" Or cut out of school, go home, and crawl under your covers. We also know what you think you might do—break into uncontrollable tears. Don't. The best thing to do is keep your cool. Take a deep breath, and let it out. Tell yourself you are going to get through this (you will) and that it has an ending (it does). (Image 5.1)

If this sounds like Mission Impossible, here's what not to do: Go to your friends when they are in a group and remind them you're not the enemy. Fair or unfair, they've already decided you are. And as we said, it's doubtful anyone will break from the group to help you. That takes guts and maturity—qualities these girls are lacking at the moment, or you wouldn't be here.

Image 5.1

Approach the girl you've angered when she is alone. She is not as likely to ignore you if she doesn't have the others backing her. Tell her you're sorry for what you did (assuming you are). Most likely, she will start talking. This is good. It's not fun, but it's conversation—and it keeps the focus between you two. Hopefully, you'll work things out at this point. If you do, tell her you're glad you resolved things, but it's important she comes to you next time she's mad—instead of involving third parties.

If you can't work things out—she ignores you or keeps yelling—walk away. Do not beg forgiveness, scream, or play victim. You'll feel stupid, and she will learn that ganging up on you helps her get her way. Keep your head up and get through the day—hour by hour. If there are others you can hang out with, do so. In the meantime, the gang will tire of treating you like a victim.

I DON'T KNOW WHAT I EVEN DID!

The only thing worse than the situation above is when you have no idea why you're being outcast. You're Target Without a Cause.

Leslie, 13, says that in her grade, it's usually fake girls who get targeted: "If a girl lies just for the sake of it, and once the word is out that she is a liar, look out. The other girls will make her miserable." She says it's especially the girls who act phony in front of guys who get it. "This one girl in my class acts all giggly and dumb in front of guys," says Leslie. "We hate her for it. We were mean to her for a few days just so she would cut it out. But of course she didn't know why she was being left out. We should have told her the reason."

Adds Tara, 12, "It's strange because it even happens to popular girls. It's like girls want to show someone who's popular what it's like to not be so popular." She also says when it comes to being dumped some girls fare better than others.

"Some girls cry or beg forgiveness. That's the worst thing to do," says Tara. "Yeah," adds Leslie, "You just look desperate." So how should you handle it? They both agree: If no one will talk to you, keep your chin up. Have a little attitude, as if you couldn't care less about their stupid game and remind yourself that it'll pass.

WHAT IF THINGS DON'T GET BETTER?

A day or two has passed, and you're still sitting by yourself at lunch. Just going to school is making you sick to your stomach, and you worry that it might never end.

Now is the time to bring in your guidance counselor, who is trained to deal with problems like this. Believe us, she's seen it before. The counselor will sit with you and hear your side of the story, and then bring in the other girls. You may feel you're tattling or making things worse. But, heck, it beats being tormented one more day. The counselor's job is to get everyone talking—and that's the first step to clearing things up.

YOU CAN BREAK THE CYCLE!

If you think, "I have never seen anything like this at my school," or "My friends would never pull something like this"—great! We wouldn't wish it on anyone. However, if in the future you are asked to join a group in shutting another person out, you'll be on guard.

You can be the one to ask the group to stop and think about what they are doing to the poor girl they are turning on. Ask them why they are exiling her and whether it's something they'll feel good about later. (If they answer yes, rest assured they'll get around to doing it to you. Run, do not walk, to a new group of girls and start making some new friends!)

If they go ahead and strike, don't play along. Not only will you feel stronger for not taking part, but your fairness will be remembered when this ridiculous war is over. You don't even need to make a big statement. Just sitting out is often good enough. In addition to winning the undying loyalty of the girl in question, others will notice your strength and courage. This will drastically cut down your own risk of attack. It's never easy to go against the group, but it sure beats going against your belief system. Here's to hoping we all can someday live in peace.

After the Blow Up

Making Up & Moving On

Image 6.1

You and your bud have made a pact to be best friends forever. You plan on buying houses next door to each other, marrying identical twins and having daughters that will be the best of friends. So why are you two no longer even speaking to each other? It happened so quickly. First, there was the out-and-out fight, when you both spewed some nasty words. Then you stopped speaking. Now you are taking the long way from homeroom to first period just to avoid passing her in the hall.

Or maybe you haven't exchanged a single hateful word—but it's obvious to you and the rest of the school that she's flat-out ignoring you. And what's really weird is that you're clueless as to why she is so ticked off.

Having a fallout with a close friend feels terrible. You may be upset, hurt, shocked or confused. If the conflict lingers, negative vibes make everyone within a five-mile radius squirm. Friction between best buds is as common as the cold and makes girls just as miserable, especially when they have no clue how to deal. Are you supposed to ignore your friend and hope the whole thing'll blow over? Should you wait for her to apologize? What if—your worst fear—she never does? As if all this weren't bad enough, you have to deal with news of The Fight spreading, causing the whole school to take sides. Could your entire social life become a casualty of friendship warfare?

In the icy aftermath of a fight, it sometimes seems that way. As painful silence stretches across hours and days, it gets harder for you and your bud to know how to stop it. But you can choose to get your relationship back on track.

FIGURE OUT WHY YOU'RE FIGHTING

If your argument is totally stupid, it's likely to blow over by itself. For example, your friend's gum cracking gets on your nerves, or she's upset you accidentally ripped her geography book cover. These issues are hardly biggies.

More serious disagreements occur when someone's genuinely upset, disappointed or hurt over something the other person said or did. Sometimes it's clear as crystal you've messed up, like when you blab a secret or badmouth a friend. If you want to make up, it's up to you to apologize and make nice.

If you're peeved 'cause your friend ignores you when her crush is around or treats you like a homework hotline, she should agree to change her ways. But it's usually not so simple. More often, it's nobody's fault, both your faults, or unclear whose fault it is. That's why it's so tricky figuring out how to fix broken friendships.

UNDERSTAND THIS MAY BE NO-FAULT

The fights that are hardest to resolve are the ones where you can't pinpoint who's right and who's wrong. Tina, 13, says her friend Bethany began ignoring her one day. "When I asked what was up, she said, 'Nothing—I'm not ignoring you.'" Tina later found out Bethany was acting strangely because another friend was angry at Tina, and Bethany "felt she had to hate me to keep that girl as a friend." Since the girls never talked it over, their friendship was severely damaged—even after Tina made up with the other girl. Tina says, "Bethany and I are no longer best buds."

Other times, after a dose of silence girls gradually start talking again. Erica, 14, reports her friend Karin was mad for an unknown reason and completely ignored her at a party. "But the next Monday, she acted as if nothing had happened." Since Erica was confused about why Karin "got mad for nothing," she says, "things haven't been the same."

Even if you and your friend can't agree, it's important to talk it through. It may seem easier to avoid each other, but ignoring small disappointments hurts a friendship. Unless you and your friend understand how each other feels, you're likely to keep upsetting each other. Also, bad feelings linger and damage trust. Instead of letting your friendship go down the tubes, try these steps:

1. Face your fears

What gets in the way of friends being straight with each other? Fear, plain and simple. Many people's worst fear is rejection. You may worry that after pouring your heart out, your best friend will continue to blow you off. Or maybe you're scared of saying what's on your mind when you're so upset. What if you don't choose the right words, or start crying and your friend laughs at you?

It's possible you won't be perfectly poised, but coach yourself to face the fear. If you break the code of silence and your pal gives you a dirty look, so what? Rejection might sting, but it is never fatal. If your friend dumps you, the friendship probably wasn't the best. So, take a deep breath and relax. The occasional spat can help you and your friend air what's been bugging you. Conflict can help you reach compromises that will strengthen your relationship, if you handle it well.

2. Make the first move

Once you get past the anxiety, it's a lot easier to gear up for a talk. Don't wait for your friend to come to you. Even if she should make the first move, does it really matter? If you let the fight fester, you both lose. If you make up, you both win. So instead of waiting for her to fix the problem, take charge.

As for timing, the sooner the better. It limits the chance everyone on the planet will dish the dirt, take sides, and make things worse. Also, the longer you wait, the more you waste on what should be awesome friendship time. If you feel too angry to approach her, take a day or two to collect your thoughts.

3. Offer the olive branch

Instead of pretending nothing happened, test the waters. Bring up the tension in a neutral way ("Hi, I miss you." "This stinks, doesn't it?" "Should we call a truce?") If you feel uncomfortable saying it to her face, slip her a message on a piece of paper with a hopeful smile.

Since everybody has different timelines for cooling off and moving past fights, remember that your style may be different from your friend's. If you get a nasty scowl in response to your kindness, don't despair. You can say, "You're still upset. When you cool off, let's talk."

Then give her space. Even though you may be eager to make up, respect your friend's need to chill. When she's ready to talk, you'll get better results.

4. Hear each other out

When you're both convinced you're right, listening to each other is tough. But how else can you find out what your friend is feeling? If needed, spell out the ground rules: "I'll listen to your view and then I'll tell you how I feel." Don't interrupt or argue while the other person is speaking.

And here's the hardest part—Listen! Think about what your friend is saying and imagine what it's been like for her. Maybe you can understand her position. Even if you didn't mean to be gossipy or exclude her, you can see why she felt that way. Hopefully, she'll do the same. That means you two respect each other.

5. Agree to disagree

Image 6.2

Sometimes, no matter how hard you try, you won't agree with your friend. She sees it one way; you see it another. It's okay that you may never see eye-to-eye, as long as you hear each other's point of view without dissing it. Agree to disagree. Then move on. Each of you can take responsibility for your part. Saying, "I'm sorry" doesn't mean you admit guilt.

Instead, it lets her know you care for her feelings. Even if you did nothing wrong, you can be sorry your friend was hurt. And you're both probably sorry the whole fight ever happened. (Image 6.2)

6. Do things differently

Can you do things differently to avoid similar fights? Maybe next time you can warn each other when you're in a bad mood or ask before borrowing stuff. You can even remember to be extra sensitive if your bud feels ignored next time you start soccer season or make a new friend at chess club.

7. Forgive each other

To rise above a fight, you must forgive. That doesn't mean forgetting what happened, but putting it in the past. As tempting as it may be to bring up the fight or rub it in, focus on the present and future. Even though it often takes a while for things to get back to normal, memories of the fight and uncomfortable feelings will fade over time.

8. Move on

Sometimes getting over a fight seems to take forever. One of you may be a world-class grudge holder. Or perhaps emotions run too high to talk things out. In these cases, ask for help. A neutral friend, counselor, teacher, or parent can help without taking sides. Working through fights is worth the trouble to keep valued friendships intact. Blow-ups, even with your best bud since kindergarten, don't have to be the end of the friendship. You have the power to put the healing process into action. And knowing how to move on after a fight leaves you confident to say what's on your mind in all of your relationships.

Bad News Buds

In that cool picture from last summer of you and your buds, you're all standing in a row, arms linked, with matching smiles and tankinis. Whether that picture lives on your dresser or only in your mind, you remember the happy feeling of being part of the group.

But things've changed since then. Your friends are exploring new paths, some of which make you not-so-comfortable. Maybe you found yourself part of a spontaneous shoplifting trip to the mall that left you wanting to crawl under the fake shrubbery. Or you may have considered moving to Bora Bora when you discovered everyone else in your group (except you, that is) was planning to cheat on the mid-terms.

Maybe it's not your whole group that's gone astray, just the one BFF who really matters. You've known her for a trillion years, but suddenly she's morphed into this, well, not exactly terrific person. You want to remain friends, but you wish she'd stop acting so high-and-mighty, weird, slutty, whatever.

As much as you'd like the power to turn everyone magically into how they used to be, you're not Sabrina. So what to do? Besides worry, that is. What

Image 7.1

follows are some answers to girls' top tricky questions about moral choices.

1. Why have things gotten so complicated? It was so simple when your biggest debate with buds was whether to play Pictionary or Monopoly. Sometimes you got your way; sometimes you didn't. But now, with friends venturing into iffy or off-limits territory, you feel pulled in different directions.

Louisa, 12, has struggled since her group started lifting stuff from the mall. "It was so great to hang with my friends without any parents around," she says, "but then it felt really weird when I realized they didn't exactly buy all the stuff they got."

When a similar thing happened to Maura, 11, she felt "like such a baby because I got so scared a cop was going to come up and arrest me. My heart started pounding so fast I almost burst out crying."

Whether your friends are sneaking around the rules, bending them a bit, or boldly smashing them to smithereens, part of you probably still wants to keep on hanging with them. You might even think they're pretty cool because they're daring or acting kind of grown up. A little thrill is not such a bad thing, right? But you don't want to get in trouble.

You also may think what they're doing is unhealthy, like smoking, or wrong. If you're associated with something a wee bit too shady for your taste, you have to deal with that awful, anxious sensation you get in your chest, like a hand squeezing your heart.

Things are complicated now because what your buds want and what you want don't always jive. This doesn't just seem complicated; it *is* complicated. So if your situation feels tough, don't beat yourself up. Give yourself a pat on the back instead for realizing you have a dilemma. It's the first step in figuring out some real solutions.

2. What's wrong with me? Of course, being part of a tight group feels terrific. If you're having a yucky day, your buds can give your self-confidence a reassuring boost. But the opposite is also true. If you're not doing what your friends are doing, you worry that there's something wrong with you. (Image 7.1)

Charlotte, 13, says, "My best friend Gia started wearing the teensiest tank tops this year. It's completely gross. But maybe I'm just jealous 'cause she has boobs or I'm just shy about my body."

"Even worse," says Tina, 14, "is when your friends start acting trashy. My close friend tells me she's been messing around with guys at parties. It's disgusting, but what if I'm just mad that nobody likes me? Maybe if I weren't a complete jerk, I'd have some fun with guys."

In every grade, it seems, girls who lead the pack often seem older and more confident than they probably actually feel inside. It's easy to think of these girls as having fun 24/7—and being way more popular than you and the others who aren't in the fast lane.

Like Charlotte and Tina, maybe you've been second-guessing yourself. Are you hopelessly uncool? Terminally infantile? Do you think that if you're different, you must be not as good? Although some girls are tempted to do "bad" things to prove they're okay or to impress their buds, this strategy is usually a dud. Ever see a girl trying too hard to wear makeup? She doesn't look glamorous—she looks clownish.

Finally, remember that social and emotional changes, like physical ones, come at different times for different girls. There's never a perfect timetable. Even if all your friends are way ahead of you, relax. Growing up is not a race, and no one is watching the clock. Years from now, no one is going to think you're awesome because you smoked a cigarette or stole a bracelet during middle school. Bottom line—if you don't feel right doing something, it's probably wrong for you. Waiting until you are ready—or deciding it'll never be right for you—is always a good thing.

3. Am I going to lose all my friends? Some girls dread being separated from their friends for a single minute, so the thought of being worlds apart is scary. You may worry that if you don't go along with the group, your buds'll kick you out.

As Mira, 13, puts it, "I'm always the one saying, 'Maybe we shouldn't,' like I'm the mother or something. Maybe they think I'm no fun anymore?"

Henny, 11, says, "Sometimes my friends are like, 'Come on, just try it.' If I say I don't want to smoke, they might not want me around." Even if your friends aren't blatantly pressuring you, you may worry that they think less of you or feel uncomfortable around you because you don't go with the flow.

Your worst fear could be that one day all your friends will drop you, and you'll be palling around with your little brother. Although we can't give you airtight guarantees, your truest bluest buds probably won't toss you off just because you say "No thanks" to something. You wouldn't have chosen such superficial clods as friends, right?

It's possible, though, that some of your friends might choose to hang out with other girls. While this may be painful, remember that it's perfectly normal for friendships to change. Circles of friends always shift as you meet new people and find you have more in common with some than others. This doesn't mean there's anything wrong with you, just that you're taking different paths.

4. Should I cover for my friend? Aaargh! You need King Solomon, or someone just as wise, to figure out what to do when a friend begs you for a favor that makes you break out in hives. Says Eghrin, 10, "My best friend was out of school for a while and had to make up a big science test, so she asked to see mine." Since Eghrin's teacher had asked everyone not to do exactly that, she was in a jam.

"I felt terrible," she says, "because she's my good friend and really needed help. Friends should help." Like Eghrin, however, you may feel torn when doing right by your friend puts you in the wrong. Eghrin realized, "Giving her the test would be the same as cheating." She also worried that helping her bud was too risky: "I know my teacher would figure out that someone showed her a test, and I could get in big trouble with the honors committee."

It's important to remember that being a good friend doesn't mean you have to violate your own values or honor code. You can choose a different path from your friend without totally abandoning her. In fact, if she's a really good bud, she will care about your feelings too. She wouldn't want you to do something that makes you feel low.

You can tell your friend you want to help her but have to find a different way. Try, "Let's see if we can think of what else will help you." In Eghrin's case, offering to tutor her friend was a workable solution. That way, she helped without compromising her honesty.

5. Should I try to change my friend? Sometimes you're truly upset about what your friend may be doing to herself. Charla, 14, was stuck with a dilemma when she learned her best friend Lizzie was riding around in cars with older boys she met at the mall.

"She's not thinking right," Charla insists. "She doesn't know these guys, and something really bad could happen to her. I don't know what to do." Basically, she struggled with whether or not she has the right to tell her friend what to do and wondered whether she could even influence her if she tried.

One option was for Charla to do nothing. She could decide that it was none of her business. Or she could consider approaching an adult (more on that later) to deal with a problem that seemed too big or too difficult. Or, and this takes guts, she could certainly bring up the situation with her friend. If that's what you choose, don't think you have to (or can) change your friend. You may just want to draw attention to the problem so she can decide for herself if she wants to change or not.

How you say your piece is critical. Compare, for example, "You're so stupid! Are you trying to get yourself killed?" with, "You know, I worry about you when you do that. Can we talk about it?" While giving advice may be tough, it's always okay to let your friend know you care about her, that you're happy to talk things over and that, if she likes, you'll be glad to help her.

Dear Carol: My best friend always brags and lies. She brags about her blond hair, grades, cheerleading, and being allowed to shave her legs. And she lied about going out with this boy. I told her I was going to ask him if it was true, and that's when she finally came clean with me. What should I do?—NON-BRAGGER

Dear Non-bragger: Sometimes people brag to cover up insecurities. When you feel great about yourself, you don't have to work hard to convince others how amazing you are. Of course, some crowing is okay. It's ideal when friends can tell each other their triumphs and setbacks. But when friends tell lies, that's a different story. Since you call this girl your best friend, let her know that you cherish her and think she's terrific, but you wish she'd be honest and wouldn't brag so much.

6. Will people think I'm bad news, too? You've probably heard a parent or grandparent say, "You're judged by the company you keep." You may have found this to be somewhat true if, say, you sit at the loudest table in the lunch room—the one that's always giving the cafeteria aide a hard time and has to be asked over and over to clean up. Even if you're the quietest girl in your group and never talk back and always bus your tray, the cafeteria aide judges you as a group. This is called "guilt by association."

Same goes for hanging with buds who get caught doing something bad. Despite your innocence, sometimes you go down too. That's a risk you take.

But it's also true that you can have a friend who flirts with calamity without being just like her. You can definitely remain your own person, even when your best bud is way different. In fact, sometimes we're attracted to people who are our opposites. We find pals who are abundant in the traits we think are decidedly lacking in ourselves.

Debbye and Randi are seventh-graders who have been friends since nursery school. While Debbye is quiet and shy, Randi is the "wild one." When they hit middle school, these differences became more exaggerated, especially around boys. At first Debbye was horrified by Randi's exploits, but now she says, "I realized I enjoy her stories. I get to have fun without actually doing that stuff myself." Like Debbye, you can learn from your friend's experiences without taking the risks. It may not be easy, but it helps to have an agreement: Don't put each other down, and respect her right to make her own choices.

7. Should I stop being friends with her? When your friend does the very thing your parents have drilled into your head not to do, you may think, "That's it. She's history. If the folks find out what she's up to, they'll put an instant kabosh on the friendship." You yourself may think this drastic solution is the only one.

Not necessarily. Rather than ditching your friend, pick and choose when and how you'll see her. Maybe you'll decide hanging in school is fine, but you won't get together afterwards. Or it's okay to invite her to your house, but not go to hers. Or you may feel comfortable being with her when adults are handy, but not at the mall or other unsupervised places. Another possibility is that you'll avoid one-on-one situations, but you'll include her when others are around.

If you've decided that none of these solutions are do-able and you definitely want to cool the friendship, you can avoid an ugly mess by doing it gradually. You don't have to stage a whole scene over it.

Branch out a little by talking to girls you don't know very well. Make plans with people you've always wanted to get together with. Avoid the temptation to tell anyone what you're doing and why. The less said, the better. That way, you're also keeping the door wide open to getting together again if you feel more comfortable hanging with her in the future.

8. What if I'm worried about my friend? Let's say your friend is doing stuff that's totally not okay—just in bad taste or wrong, but possibly dangerous. Beyond deciding to avoid the activity yourself, what should you do?

Miranda, 13, became worried about a friend who was drinking from her parents' liquor cabinet. Miranda wasn't sure if her friend was "just experimenting" or "had a problem." If you find yourself wondering whether your friend's behavior is normal or scary, it's a good idea to ask an adult for some advice.

You can't expect to know all the answers. So talk to a parent, school guidance counselor, or trusted teacher. If you're concerned about your friend's privacy, don't give her name. The important thing is that you and an adult figure out a way to get your friend help if she needs it. She may not appreciate it at first, but that's being a good friend.

Branching Out

Make New Friends But Keep the Old You

Just before the clock struck midnight on New Year's Eve, Melissa made a promise to herself this would be the last year she'd spend without a ton of friends. Melissa swore that she'd be one of the few, the chosen—the popular.

And Melissa wasn't sitting idle, waiting for her fairy godmother to come along and wave her magic wand. She took back all the teddy-bear sweatshirts her grandma gave her for Christmas and bought some cool new jeans. The money she earned baby-sitting was invested in a great haircut. She even took the new diary her mom gave her and used it to record goals for her new and improved self. She vowed to make one cool new bud every month. "It won't be hard," she thought. "I can be friendly, and the cheerleading tryouts for basketball are just around the corner. Lots of cool girls are on the squad." Melissa was sure she was destined for social success.

So how did the year go for Melissa?

"Awful," groans Melissa, now 12, looking back. "I thought that by looking like the girls who are popular, making the cheerleading squad and doing what they

Image 8.1

did, the cool girls would accept me. And a few of them did. For a couple of months there, things were going according to my plans."

Melissa shouldn't have been surprised. It's not that she didn't know how to be a good friend—she did. Matter of fact, Melissa had two great friends *before* she decided to change her persona. Sara, also 12, had been her best friend since third grade. And her next door neighbor Sam was someone Melissa could always count on for a quick game of hoops, or for help with memorizing those history dates.

"When I came to school that first day after Christmas break, Sara said she didn't even recognize me. And it wasn't just my clothes and hair. I thought I had to act like a snob, too. I saw that some popular girls excluded people, so I thought my first step should be to snub my old friends in favor of new ones. I really hurt Sara."

Even Sam, her trusty guy pal, was confused. "One day, Melissa was on my driveway playing basketball with me, the next, all she wanted to do was bounce around and yell for guys on the team. I never got it. Heck, she could beat half of the guys on the basketball court."

Thinking back is harder for Sara, "I knew what Melissa was doing. Both of us used to sit around and think how great it would be to be popular. But she treated me like dirt, so I made friends with this girl who likes to write and act, like Melissa and I used to. After a while, it was fun to have new friends, and I assumed Melissa was having fun with her new friends, too." (Image 8.1)

But it wasn't long before Melissa's new "popularity" came crashing down. "As soon as basketball ended," says Melissa, "so did my new social life. The girls I had been hanging out with sort of faded away. By that time, Sara had a new friend and Sam stuck to hanging out with the guys. I was left alone. And that's when I realized that even though I looked and acted like a popular girl—and, in a way, hung out with them—I wasn't really their friend and they weren't mine. Like when they would talk to me on the bus on the way to games, they were just chatting. I took it to mean they were interested. But all of those girls already had friends. They really didn't see me as part of their group."

After spending a few lonely weeks trying to figure out what went wrong, Melissa called Sara and Sam. Many long talks, apologies, and a little time later, things went back to normal. "I still like my haircut, and I wear those new clothes to the mall, but when it comes to friends, I am happiest with Sara and Sam."

At some point or another, each of us resolves to get out there and make new friends. That's perfectly natural, and it's always great to find new people who are fun to be around. But like anything else, making lots of new friends is a skill. Just like you might be good at basketball or writing, some people are good at making friends. They have what experts call "social skills." Popular people have skills that *get* them friends, skills which are different from the skills you need to *be* a good friend.

As Melissa found out, people aren't well-liked just because they have the right clothes or hair or do a certain activity. Take a good look around your school, and you'll notice that all kinds of people have tight groups of friends. Funny girls, athletic girls, girls who act and create art—all have their own fun social scenes. Maybe in your school, "being popular" means hanging out with a certain person or glamorous clique. But again, as Melissa learned, these connections hardly guarantee you a hopping good time. A truly awesome social life means having good friends that share your interests, or support you and your beliefs, or make you laugh, or help you create. Or all of the above. Or whatever you think is important. Melissa wasn't wrong for trying to expand her social life. While some girls crave just a few tight buds to hang out with, other girls prefer being friends with lots of different people. Talking to people with various opinions and backgrounds opens your mind to all sorts of amazing ideas and activities. Who could blame anyone for wanting that?

Melissa's big mistake was the way she went about making new friends. Dropping old friends for new ones is incredibly lame, and so is picking friends based on how good it might look to be seen with them. So what's the right way to add new friends to your life?

What follows are some hints to help you make all the new friends you want. We've all heard about being friendly (say "hi!") and open (get involved!). What follows are the less obvious tips for making new friends.

Hint #1: Pick the right people. We know—we said it's not the people that make you popular. The point is to pick people you have stuff in common with. It's not so much that the popular basketball cheerleaders snubbed Melissa. They just realized something that Melissa didn't—they had absolutely no mutual interests past the pom-poms.

You can have some people as "friends," some as "good friends," and some as "best friends." You can also have "math class friends," "youth group friends," even a "friend who will watch X Files without screaming uncontrollably and having nightmares afterward." It's great to have a mix, especially if you get a kick out of people with different interests. But the truth is that unless you have a few things in common, things get boring—fast.

When you do find girls with a shared interest (it's not that hard), it's a plus if they like to make new friends too. Some "popular" people create that illusion by excluding others. But some are just "people" people who are always looking to make new buds. They are usually the ones who are eager to organize your team's fund-raising bake sales, host scenery-painting parties for the school play, and lead the student council. Since doing their thing requires the help of others, they'll be as into meeting you as you are into meeting them. Even if you don't become new best friends with them, they might bring you into a group where you will make another connection.

Dear Carol: Some girls in my class are really preppy and rich and they have big houses and wear new clothes. They are nice to me and say hi and stuff, but sometimes I think they are laughing behind my back.—LESS LUCKY

Dear Less Lucky: No matter how much you have, there is always someone out there who has more. Rather than dwell on what others have, you're better off looking at what *you* have. Do you have a loving family? Are you rich in friends? What are your special talents? You say you are less lucky, but money is not the only measurement. I doubt these girls are laughing at you any more than you would laugh at a girl whose home is smaller than yours.

Hint #2: Pace yourself. Another one of Melissa's mistakes was to push things too quickly. Unless you are starting over at a new school, you really should take this new friend thing slowly. Like it or not, people have a certain image of you, and if you do a 180-degree turnaround, everyone will wonder what's up. One day you're Susie Smith, next you're Miss All-That.

Better to be yourself with some frosting. Think about the last time you were in a really killer mood, right after you aced a test or scored the winning goal. Remember how you felt like you could do anything, talk to anybody, and it didn't matter if the cutest guy in school said hi back or not? Try to project a bit of that infectious spirit every day. Yes, some days are hard enough to get through without trying to be perky on top of it. But it's worth the effort.

Instead of thinking you are a kiss-up, new people will notice your good mood. And people like to surround themselves with people who are positive—that's how life goes. While you don't want to be totally fake (people don't expect you to crack jokes if your dog just died), you do want to put your best face forward. There will be enough time later for your new friend to help your lows as well as share your highs.

Hint #3: Learn to read. No, not Shakespeare—body language. This is a difficult thing to learn and takes some practice. But it's the thing experts say separates the socially skilled from the rest of us. By watching people's faces, expressions, posture, and body positions, you can tell how they are reacting to you.

You probably already have some experience picking up subtle clues. If your mom slams the door on her way in and smacks the grocery bags on the counter, chances are this isn't the right time to ask if you can have a friend over for dinner. That's body language. (Image 8.2)

Image 8.2

But often, when we try to make a good impression we focus so much on what we are saying and doing that we forget about the person we're trying to impress in the first place! Smiles are an easy way to tell if someone is into you. But is that smile real? Nervous? Do her eyes say one thing and her face another? Every few minutes, check out the facial expression of the person you're chatting with. Is she giving you her rapt attention? Or looking down the hall?

And while you have to start a friendship somewhere (talking about the weather counts), try not to make too much out of first encounters. Every once in a while, you'll instantly hit it off with someone, but most people will be a bit reserved until they get to know you better. Respect that distance, and keep things quick and light for a while.

Hint #4: Keep some mystery. It's hard to resist the temptation to spend every waking moment with a new friend. You want to share everything with her. But some people feel overwhelmed by so much instant attention, so don't Krazy Glue yourself to her.

Plus, you don't want her to think you had no life before. Keep up with old friends (oh, by the way, did we mention that only the lowest of the low dump their old friends while making new ones?), practice your flute, write a play, whatever. As the comedian Groucho Marx once said "I don't want to belong to any club that would have me as a member." As odd as that sounds, remember that most people are suspicious of anything that comes too easily. If you are desperate to be friends with someone, that person will pick up those vibes. And, let's face it, no one wants to hang out with someone who comes off as being really needy. So enjoy your budding friendships, but also keep other interests kicking.

Hint #5: Consider doing the unexpected. Don't have much in common with the masses? While it's great to be the golden girl, some people just aren't comfortable in groups or don't find what they are looking for in clubs or sports. So, why not start your own club? Girls who enjoy writing may find themselves solo a lot more than they like. Instead of going it alone, why not start a writers' workshop? Get together with other scribes to talk about your writing.

Computer-savvy girls also spend mucho screen time alone, but that's when on-line chat rooms come in handy. Having an e-mail buddy is tons of fun, even if you just send silly lists or poetry to each other. So, even if your passion tends to require a lot of alone time, don't give up on friendships. Use your hobby in a creative way to connect with like-minded souls.

Don't like organized groups? There is another option. It's called being friends with everyone. Literally. Some girls are uncomfortable with the pressure of being a best friend or find that belonging to a clique is super limiting. Like Switzerland, you can become a country that doesn't take any one side, yet remains a part of the big picture. By being friends with everyone, you can play Sega with the guys, hang at the mall with the mallrats, be in a play with the drama gang, and then play tennis on the team. While this may sound like the perfect solution, it's not for girls who need a lot of security. Often girls in these situations are extremely self-reliant and have no problem relating to anyone. They are social chameleons. But if that's you, this is the way to go.

Hint #6. Don't forget the basics. Have something to talk about, be it the latest movie or what you did over the weekend. Be supportive when someone needs it. Be a good student (no one wants to hang out with troublemakers—detention is not cool). Really listen to what other people are saying, and resist the temptation to hog the spotlight, even if you think you have a million great stories to tell. And finally—yep, we'll say it—be yourself. As Melissa found out, pretending to like being a basketball cheerleader is a lot harder than playing basketball: "The whole time I've played basketball, no one ever asked me to do splits." Aaarghh!

How to Be a Happy Camper

About all you need to pack for summer camp are T-shirts, shorts, bug spray, and sunscreen. Wish you could pack your BFFs, too? Not so fast. "Even though I only have a few weeks with my friends from camp, those are some of the best weeks of my year—and some of the best friends I have," says Madison, 11. While it might seem easier to hide under the nearest swim dock instead of mustering up the guts to introduce yourself to complete strangers, almost every happy camper we know has this advice: "Just do it! Everyone else is there to make friends, too." Here are some tried-and-camp-tested hints to get the ball rolling. (Image 9.1)

Image 9.1

Just say hi. "Walk over to the person and say, 'Hi! My name is [your name here]. What's yours?' Sounds simple but it works."—CHARITY

Find an icebreaker. "I was waiting for a hot dog with another girl, and the guy making them was taking his time. So I turned to her and said, 'We're not the only ones on vacation here!' She laughed, and I introduced myself."—JENNA

Don't limit yourself. "Don't dismiss a girl just because she isn't the type of person you would normally spend time with. Try to find common interests, and accept generosity. Be open and honest, and let other girls know they can be open and honest with you."—LUCY

Get involved. "Focus on having a great time. Be yourself, but don't be the one who never wants to do what the group is doing. Take part in activities and compromise."—EMILY

Be friendly, and put the other person first. "You can make a person feel really good by making her the subject of your sentence. Try my trick. Instead of saying something like, 'I love your sweater!' say, 'You look great in that.' That puts the focus on your new friend."—TARA

Be courageous. Jenna, who shared her icebreaker, reminds herself that if someone isn't friendly back, it probably has nothing to do with her: "I say in my head, 'I don't sound like a dork; I sound friendly.' After all, what would I think if someone tried to be nice to me? I'd think she was pretty cool!"

The Girls' Life

Guide to Family

Battle of the Sibs

Image 10.1

Some days you're sure your sib was put on this planet strictly to annoy you. Unfortunately, brothers and sisters know just which buttons to push to make each other certifiably crazy. Does any of the following sound familiar?

"I'll flip if my sister barges into my room one more time, steals any more of my stuff, or butts in at the exact moment I'm spilling a story to my friends."—NAT, 12

"My brother only needs to hear the tires of my parents' car leaving the driveway to start busting on me. Then he moves onto teasing, followed by insults, and finally onto name-calling that's so mean I burst into tears."—JENNI, 11 (Image 10.1)

"My so-called sister thinks the best way to handle battles is pushing, pinching, and shoving. I'm sick of being on guard all the time and feeling absolutely powerless."—BETHANY, 15

"Fights with my brother start over the remote, which video we watch, or whose turn it is to be on-line. It's like summer reruns—we have the same scenes over and over."—MELISSA, 14

In most cases, it's not that your sib is a 24/7 nightmare. You probably have some moments when you don't think your baby sister should be stuffed inside her bedroom closet for all of eternity. You probably even enjoy your big bro's company from time to time. And you may be capable of seeing the positive side of having sisters and brothers, like having a sidekick for car rides and rainy days, and that essential extra player for two-person PlayStation games.

"My younger sister Melanie does worship me and can be downright cute ... well, when she's asleep," admits Cari, 10. Older sibs can drive you to the mall and give advice on how to cope with, say, the same treacherous teacher they had in middle school. Big sisters occasionally loan you clothes and earrings (not the primo stuff, of course). Brothers bring their very fine friends right to your front door.

"The benefits sometimes make up for the bothering, bickering, and other bad scenes," says Lani, 15. But more than a few girls tell us their home turf is a battleground in need of a United Nations peace-keeping force. The worst fights seem to start when girls are forced to fend off hostile sibs alone—without adults to intervene and referee. "It's like combating bullies at school, sometimes worse," reports Mia, 13.

Since so many parents work, lots of girls have to take care of themselves—and sometimes younger sibs—after school and into the early evening. And your folks probably expect you guys to be okay on your own while they run errands. That's dandy—that is, if you don't routinely serve as your sib's number one punching bag. But if you draw battle lines the second the 'rents hit the road, being parentless for even a half-hour is torture. To exterminate the pestering, we'll help you figure out what might be causing all the conflicts and outline some tactics for turning war into peace.

There are as many reasons for sib fights as there are sibs. Sometimes, there doesn't even seem to be a reason. That's just the way you relate to each other. You speak to each other with an edge in your voice or an obnoxious tone you wouldn't dare use with anyone else. You tease or belittle each other out of sheer habit. Or, as Christina, 10, says, "We're just taking our anger out on each other."

When you're frustrated or upset about overdue book reports, backstabbing friends, or detention (again), it's easy to lash out at the nearest target—a sib. Plus, it's a pain sharing space with people whose habits may pluck your nerves. Add normal feelings, like jealousy and competition, and you have kindling for rip-roaring sibling blowouts.

And don't dismiss good old sibling rivalry. One 11-year-old reader, whose 14-year-old sister regularly picks fights, says, "I think she secretly envies me because I go to the mall a lot with my friends, get invited to parties, get good grades, and am better at sports." Whether it's school performance, appearance, social status, whatever, if your sib is sure she's a dark shadow compared to your ray of light, she'll probably attempt to even the playing field the first chance she gets.

It's doubtful you've sat around just whining, hiding, or hoping your sib will get bored harassing you. Instead, you've likely tried a tactic or two or three that just hasn't done the trick.

While the folks might tell you to just ignore taunting sibs, that strategy (as you know all too well) almost always fails. Nicki, 13, says, "When my brother starts in with me, I don't even look at him or answer him back. My mom says if I ignore him, he'll realize he doesn't get to me and will lose interest. But it just makes him hotter, and he doesn't let up until he gets a reaction out of me."

Keeping to yourself in your room or basement or attic is also usually a no-win. "If I'm home, my sister always finds me," says Henny, 11. And you've definitely told your offending sib to cut it out so many times that it falls on deaf ears. No wonder you feel helpless! What you need are time-tested strategies that will absolutely obliterate the problem. Take your pick from the arsenal that follows.

Dear Carol: My sister is 17 and she's always on the phone, in the shower or out. She used to like being with me.—SAD SIS

Dear Sister: Tell her you miss her. Make popcorn and knock on her door to confide in her or ask her advice about a friend. Or leave a note under her pillow saying, "Let's go for a walk this weekend." Or draw a picture of the two of you and slip it under her door. If you gently remind her that you're still around, she may be happy to include you once in a while. Even if she is busier than ever, I bet she still likes being with you.

Choose your battles wisely. If you get caught up in petty problems—like your sister took a bracelet or your brother gets to sit in the front of the car—you and your sib will be in combat virtually all the time. Who needs that? Instead, decide what you can live with and what you can't.

Maybe you can tolerate your brother controlling the stereo when your parents are out—but you can't deal with him barging into your room. Or you can stand the teasing, but not the arm-twisting. Sit down with your sib when things are peaceful and a parent is around. Relay your message simply, clearly, and firmly: "Look, from now on, I'm not going to stand for this" Don't whine, threaten, beg or cajole. Just say it—and mean it.

Do your part. As tempting as it may be to blame your sibling for 100 percent of the problem, that's often unfair. Ask yourself, honestly, how you may contribute. Julia, 12, thinks her sister is perpetually peeved with her. Julia admits, however, that she constantly goes into her sister's room and "borrows" her newest clothes without permission.

If Julia changes her behavior—like by asking first—her sister may get less ticked and won't be as likely to retaliate. Sounds simple, but seeing that you're making an effort might be all your sib needs to cool the crossfire from her side.

Another example? Suppose you tattle on your brother (the one who thinks he's so cool and superior) just because it's fun to see him crash and burn. You may win the battle—but once you guys are alone you may be in for some ancient Chinese torture treatment. Is it worth it? We don't think so.

Resist being baited. Sibs are masters at knowing precisely how to make you go ballistic. Then, when you lose control and swear at them or take a swing, they use your reaction as an excuse for beating you up or getting you grounded. As Lyndsey, 11, reports, "When your sis or bro lies, accuses you of something you didn't do or says rude things, it's easy to retaliate." But losing it is precisely what they want you to do.

Instead of taking the bait, stay cool-headed. Distracting your sib ("Why don't we see if we can program the VCR?") sometimes works, too. Amy, 13, suggests going to your room, putting on headphones, reading, or thinking about something else. Do anything to resist spewing words or actions that will infuriate your sib and, therefore, backfire.

Make a pact. Draw up a peace treaty. Promise not to do the three things that most annoy your sib as long as he agrees not to do whatever bugs you. This can be applied to attitudes (no overprotectiveness or bossiness), aggression (no hitting or tickling), or annoying habits (no borrowing stuff or tattling).

Maybe your big bro is mad about having to be in charge when your parents step out because you always make a huge mess. Offer to organize the cleanup if he stops barking orders.

Call in the reinforcements. Your parents may tell you not to tattle—and you may fear things will get worse if you blow the whistle. But if you are being hurt or feel truly frightened, you must tell an adult. Even if your mom and dad have told you not to interrupt them at work, don't hesitate to pick up the phone in serious situations. But there's a huge difference between getting your mom out of a meeting to say, "Steven won't let me watch my show," and, "Steven sprained my left arm." Tell your mom it's important, and then describe exactly what's going on.

Dear Carol: My brother is in tenth grade and obsessed with girls. He's always on the phone with them, and he's never nice to me. He was never mean to me before he got obsessed with girls. I feel like I'm losing my brother. Can you help?—SCORNED SISTER

Dear Scorned: Ouch! Who needs a nasty brother when you had a nice one? What to do? You could yell at your brother to stop yelling at you, but that never works. How about inviting him to do something fun, or sending him a note saying you miss him? That should turn him around. Also explain to him that girls like guys who are kind to their siblings. And be patient. Girlfriends come and go, but brothers and sisters stay in each other's lives forever.

When your parents get home from work, ask for some discussion time ASAP. Tell them what's been going down and that you need help. Hopefully, they will respond seriously. If not, tell another trusted adult, such as a relative, teacher or counselor. You have a right to feel safe.

Life is peachier when you and your sibs get along peacefully. You'd love for even one day to hang out in the living room without worrying about being taunted, teased, or put into a headlock. As impossible as this may seem, it will more than likely happen down the road. Okay, so it might not happen until your big brother leaves for Dartmouth. But don't give up hope.

In the meantime, take positive steps toward getting along. And when your sib eventually treats you with respect, appreciate it. It may be the start of a beautiful friendship.

Superstar Sibs

How to Reclaim Some of That Spotlight

You're somewhat athletic, nice enough, and you've certainly got one or two things you're pretty good at. But you're no superstar. Unlike, say, your brother or sister, whose radiance seems to shine all over the entire house—he's a star soccer player, or she's a piano prodigy. Many girls with superstar siblings wish they, too, could be ultra special, or even noticed—as in, "Hel-lo? Remember me?" It can be positively miserable living in the lonely, dark space of someone else's shadow. But that doesn't have to be your destiny. No matter what type of attention-getter your sib is, you don't have to let his or her star status shrink your own self-esteem.

THE TALENT

Sibling stars come in dozens of varieties. Crystal's sister Leah is the state tennis champ. Crystal, 11, says, "Dinner conversations are always about Leah's last win, her next tournament, how she'll train, blah, blah, blah." Crystal is quick to point out that her parents also ask about her activities and include her in conversations, "but which is more exciting—my A on a history quiz, or Leah's win in her age division? Sure, they might say, 'Way to go,' when I get a good grade, but big deal. Our family room looks like a showroom with all of Leah's ribbons and trophies." But the worst part, according to Crystal, is "being dragged all over the place, to this tournament, that exhibition—sometimes all weekend long. It's not even for me!"

It's not that Crystal has anything against tennis. In fact, she thinks playing with her friends might be fun—but she doesn't even try because, "I'd feel like a dufus when Leah's so great at it." So how does Crystal deal with her sister's success? "I try really hard to be happy for her," she says, "I mean, she is my sister. But sometimes I just want to scream, 'You know what? I don't even care about your stupid matches or your stupid victories!'"

YOU'RE HER SISTER?

Some sibs don't even have to have any talent to shine. They have looks that people think are perfect, and they don't have to do a darn thing. Says Janine, 15, "Having a younger sister who looks like a fairy princess is a major drag. Alessandra's so gorgeous that wherever we go, people stare and smile. I swear, I could fall down and die, and nobody'd notice! Sometimes, people say, 'You don't look anything like your sister,' and I say, 'Gee, thanks.'" It doesn't help that, unlike Janine, Alessandra loves the frilly, fussy clothes their mom picks out. While Janine's wardrobe is confined to the few items she and her mom can agree on, "Alessandra goes through major costume changes." (Image 11.1)

Image 11.1

For a while, Janine tried to copy Alessandra's look but eventually gave up. "Alessandra is just lucky—she has the perfect hair, sparkly blue eyes, pearly teeth. How can I compete with that?"

What did Janine do? "I went the total opposite direction," she confesses, "I stopped taking care of myself." In the past year, Janine quit eating healthy foods, gave up her dance class, and gained fifteen pounds. Now Janine's sloppy appearance makes such a statement that she, too, draws stares—and not very complimentary ones.

Several factors can make sibling stars even less bearable:

IF NOT BEST, FIRST

Many girls feel it's far worse when a younger sibling leaves them in the dust in a meteoric rise to glory. There's an unwritten law that says older sibs hit milestones first. They're supposed to master long division, learn the butterfly, and get braces off before the younger sib. So if little sis steals your thunder by getting the first bra or going on the first date, the universe may seem out of whack. "To be honest, I wanted to strangle Lisa," says Cindi, 14. "She developed way before me and pranced around in a bikini all summer. I was so humiliated I stayed away from the pool as much as I could."

SOMETHING ABOUT SISTERS

When younger brothers beat girls on the lifeguard test or master black-diamond slopes before them, they may feel un-special, but usually less murderous. No doubt about it, most girls agree that having a star sister is significantly worse torture than having a star brother.

Why? For starts, comparing ourselves to other girls seems automatic. The thinking goes, "We're both girls, so we should be equally good at (acing tests/scoring goals/making guys drool, whatever.)" With brothers, on the other hand, girls can take the sting out of their achievements with consolations such as "He's got the genes," or "He's been allowed to do stuff first," or "He and Dad have a male bonding thing." As Becca says, "Tim is built like a football player, so it makes sense that he excels at sports that take a lot of strength."

AND YOU DO WHAT?

When the star sibling's interests and talents mimic those of a parent, this can also make girls more inclined to hate-filled fantasies. Take Melody, 12, whose younger sister, Jill, goes golfing with their dad every Saturday. "The first time he took Jill out, he said, 'She's a natural.' I got the Fisher-Price plastic clubs, and she got real ones," says Melody. "I hate the fact that she and my dad are like best friends now. It's not my fault I'm not good at golf."

KEEPING SCORE

So where does all this leave you? We have a news bulletin: Having a star sibling has no effect on your own potential—really. It's not luminous sibs themselves, but rather the need to compete with them that does girls in. Once you truly accept this, you'll find time to focus on your own life! What your sister or brother does—or doesn't do—has absolutely no bearing on what *you* can do.

A sib who scores home runs, for example, has no effect on your own RBI or potential to make team captain. If your sib is a concert pianist, you can still play for fun—or be a concert pianist yourself. Contrary to popular opinion, there aren't limits on "smart genes" or "sports genes" in each family. Who you are is up to you.

So why is the need to be best so strong? Deep down, the real question may be, "Do my parents love my sibling more than they love me?"

As Crystal says, "Every time Leah brings home a tennis trophy, I get a sick feeling and think, 'How can I compete with that?' Then I tell myself I don't have to." Although there are rare exceptions, most parents have enough love for all their children, regardless of how they look or what they accomplish.

FACING REALITY

No, you may never dive as well as your dolphin-like brother or sing like your soprano sister. And you know, there will always be super-whatevers who are prettier, smarter, or more talented than you and everybody else. But just because a girl in skating class glides like Michelle Kwan, do you unlace and vacate the ice? Ofcourse not. Even though you can't be tops, you should never stop being your best or simply enjoying an activity.

There are certain factors you can't change. Older sibs will usually drive first, date before you, and get more privileges. You have to deal. Besides, think of the advantages of your sibling position (they've paved the way, you get rides, etc.). Don't automatically assume your sib gets things because he or she is a star. You may get hand-me-downs while your sister sports brand-new trendy clothes simply because an older sister may grow faster or develop first.

NOTHING'S PERFECT

Thinking your sibs (and their lives) are perfect is a huge mistake. No such thing, sis. It's easy to think a sister who brings home straight A's or a brother who stars on every team has an enchanted life. But being good at one thing doesn't mean everything comes easily. Many star sibs have their own struggles.

Jen, 12, whose 11-year-old sister Monica's math talent is a constant source of irritation, admits that Monica has trouble making friends: "She really relates better to numbers than people."

Being a star also means sacrifices—missed parties, mall trips, and other fun stuff. Being a ranked tennis player is cool but, says Crystal's sister Leah, "Sometimes I just want a normal life—you know, hang out, go to movies, shop. At school, I'm not sure people like me for me or because I'm in the paper." The flip side to fame is also tremendous pressure to perform. Stars may even be expected to "set an example."

When we asked Leah if she thinks about how her star status affects Crystal, she sighed and said, "I feel bad that Crystal is dragged around to tournaments. I know she hates it. But I wish she understood that tennis can be grueling, especially all the pressure I feel to win. She seems to think my life is blessed."

Seeing the universe from your sib's point of view may help you see fame as less enviable and maybe even lonely. See, stardom doesn't guarantee happiness.

FINDING YOUR OWN SPARKLE

In a misguided belief that "If I can't be 'the best' I won't even try," many girls neglect activities, schoolwork, or appearance. But you don't have to set lofty goals or be the best. Just be you. If bowling, writing poetry, or taking guitar lessons seem fun, go ahead. So what if they seem unglamorous or aren't prize-oriented? Or you may be good at taking chances, have a way with animals, or be capable of surfing the Net. While these qualities seldom win awards, they do bring significant rewards.

REMEMBER ME?

No matter what you do, things aren't always "fair." Sometimes, parents devote more time, money and attention to you, other times to sibs. Hopefully, your parents will treat you each as an individual who needs specific things at specific times. Just like kids, however, parents may need reminders. If you want more attention, you might have to ask for it. Try "I'd like to spend some alone time with you. When could we have an hour together?" Recognize that your special time might have to be arranged around your sib's games, performances, or schedule.

If you still feel lost in the shuffle, you might need to ask your parents to make as big a fuss over your achievements as your sib's. If parents compare you to your sib, point out that you're trying your best. And as long as you really are, you'll light up any room.

You Say Potato, I Say...

Are You and Mom Like Night and Day?

The woman is driving you batty. Yes, she's your mom and you love her to pieces, but sometimes you'd swear you were switched at birth with some other baby in the hospital. How could this person who's responsible for half your genetic makeup have seemingly nothing in common with you? How can your appearances, personalities and/or preferences be so totally opposite? More important, how are you supposed to get along with her when your differences seem like a canyon that can't be bridged? She can't even relate to the things that matter most to you.

If you and your mom seem like night and day, you're hardly alone. Most girls, in fact, find that they part ways with their moms on at least one if not a ton of important issues. And while you think life would be easier if you and your mom were two peas in a pod, you should know that your differences don't necessarily spell disaster. In fact, with an open mind and a bit of effort, you two can learn to tolerate, respect and—believe it or not—even appreciate each other's uniqueness.

HOW DIFFERENT ARE YOU TWO?

When it comes to answering this question, some girls don't even know where to start. Addie, 14, for instance, only half-jokingly asks, "You got a couple days? My mom and I are nothing alike. We look different, we act different, and we think differently." Says Mika, 14, "My friends don't believe it when they meet my mother. I like wearing jeans and sweat shirts, playing sports, and getting messy. All she cares about is shopping and makeup and looking perfect."

For other girls, the differences between them and their moms aren't as overwhelming. Jill, 11, focuses mostly on the physical, "My mom is tall and blond and I'm short and dark," she says. But when asked about stuff that's more than skin deep, Jill adds, "I guess we both like to do outdoor stuff, like hiking and biking, and we also care about animals a lot."

The truth is, it's probably impossible to find any two people whose looks, tastes and habits are perfectly the same. You and your mom are no exception. But maybe it's not the actual differences that you mind. Maybe what you can't stand is your mom's disapproval of these differences. Whenever you don't agree on something, she's convinced her opinion's right. This is a major problem because

100

your mom, after all, gets the final word on what you do.

Fourteen-year-old Alexis adds, "I'm sick of my mom trying to make me a little version of herself. I just want to be me!" Although you can't make your mom enjoy the things you do, you can figure out ways to make life more bearable despite your separate tastes. Let's break them down by issue. Below are the ones that seem to spark the most frequent mother-daughter clashes. (Image 12.1)

Image 12.1

TWO SHIPS PASSING...

Some of us are "morning people," while others of us live and breathe for the snooze button. These aren't things we can change at will, they're just quirks and characteristics that make up our personalities.

Marta, 11, says, "Living with my stepmom is torture. I can't sleep in on weekends because she's up at dawn doing chores and making a racket. All I want to do is get some sleep." Things get pretty heated because Marta's step-mom keeps telling Marta she doesn't pitch in enough; Marta is infuriated because she doesn't see why her chores can't wait until later when she wakes up. "I would help her," Marta claims, "but by the time I get up, she says it's too late!"

Natalie, 13, reports the reverse situation. "My mom goes to bed practically right after dinner. She's always yelling, 'Light's out!' and 'Be quiet!' I can't help it if my friends call at nine and wake her up. My schedule is normal, hers isn't."

These conflicts happen because people—and that includes moms and daughters—are born with distinct biorhythms which, at times, don't mesh. Since this can happen between sisters sharing a bedroom and even roommates in boarding school, it's important to learn how to cope.

First, realize that nobody's at fault here. Rather than blaming each other, use that energy to admit that differences exist and find workable compromises. For example, Natalie and her mother agreed to accept calls until 9P.M. and then to turn off the phone's ringer. Marta and her stepmom figured out a schedule that allowed her a few extra zzzzs in the A.M. and yet enough time to make a dent in the laundry pile. She and her step-mom both felt less resentful and more content.

THE TWINKIE ZONE

Dinnertime can really bring out the differences in people. Danielle, 13, says she used to love her mother's cooking until she lived on a farm last summer. "Ever since then, I can't look at the stuff my mom makes, much less eat little chicks or piglets." Danielle's mom hasn't taken too kindly to her daughter giving the thumbs down to meat. "She's really judging me," Danielle complains. "She's telling me I'm just being difficult, like I'm doing it on purpose or something. But I'm not."

Snacks are yet another biggie. Some girls prefer snacking to eating, which drives their mothers wild. "My mother's always telling me I'm 'ruining my appetite' when I make myself a mini-pizza or grilled cheese in the afternoon. But who cares if I'm not hungry for dinner? Just because she likes a huge meal at the end of the day doesn't mean I have to."

It's important to make sure that battles over food are really about food. If you're upset with your mom about something else, deal with that issue directly. If it's truly a question of different tastes in food, you and your mom can deal with that. You might go through some cookbooks together and find meals that appeal to everyone. She might agree to cook your favorite meal once a week. Or you might learn to cook a few of your favorite dishes for your whole family. Chances are, your food likes and dislikes will change a zillion times in the next few years. Just make sure you're not making a fuss about dinner to make a point about something else, and your mom's not taking your pickiness personally.

CLASHES OVER CLOTHES

Another topic that often sends girls and moms spinning into different directions is clothes. Let's face it, the days of Laura Ashley matching mother/daughter outfits are way way behind you. You're enjoying experimenting with clothes and finding your own unique style. So what's the problem with having your own look?

The problems begin, girls say, when mothers balk at their daughters' choice of clothing. Margaret, 13, reports "I guess my style is just too much for my mom. She's so stuffy that she freaks out when I wear anything she considers too tight. She keeps saying my outfits are 'inappropriate' and making me change my clothes. What does she want me to wear? Turtlenecks in July?"

Okay, let's make a distinction here: having different taste from your mom is one thing, having poor taste is another. It's crucial that you and your mom discuss and define the difference for yourselves. When your choice of clothes isn't too skimpy, suggestive or offensive—but merely a matter of preference—perhaps you and your mom can agree to disagree.

This strategy worked well for Tamara, also 13. "My mom wears these flowy long dresses that make her look like a hippie from the 60s, and I dress pretty preppie. People think we look weird together, but it really doesn't bother us."

Accepting differences in style goes both ways. Next time your mom shows up in an atrocious straw hat, you may just have to clamp your lips. In fact, to avoid ugly scenes and hurt feelings, why not make a pact with your mother? You'll both accept the fact that from time to time (or every day, in some cases), your outfits will make each other cringe. But no matter what, you won't insult, tease, or critique the other. In fact, maybe you won't even hint about the merits of each other's accessories—unless specifically asked.

MUSIC TO WHOSE EARS?

It's hard even to imagine a daughter and mom agreeing on music. In fact, moms sometimes insist their daughters' musical tastes are designed to give them migraines. Debby, 13, says "I'm really into Fiona Apple, but whenever I listen to it, my mom asks me, 'Can't you find a CD that's not so dark and intense?' She thinks the words are too angry, but that doesn't mean I should." Sam, 12, has a similar complaint. "My mom likes music like Simon and Garfunkel—oldies and stuff, which she plays real low. So when my music's at normal volume, she freaks and tells me to turn it down." These situations call for immediate negotiation and compromise that both of you can live with—before hard feelings accumulate. And a good set of earphones might be a lifesaver for everyone.

Moms and daughters disagree not just on what kind of music and how loudly it's played, but also on when and how much girls listen. Lauren, 11, likes background music when she does homework and falls asleep. "My mom doesn't understand how I can do two things at once. But listening to music actually helps me." You may need to demonstrate how music affects you. For example, Lauren's mother backed off when she showed her mother her solid homework record and proved she could wake up on time on school mornings.

Why not take the approach "Different strokes for different folks?" Maybe you can describe to your mom what you think your music says and why you like it. You probably won't convert her, but it might help her to be more tolerant. And the next time some sappy love song your mom loves comes on the car radio, don't pretend to hurl or change the station. Fair is fair.

PARTY ANIMAL VS. COUCH POTATO

Yet another potential danger zone is personality. Katelyn, 12, describes herself as pretty soft-spoken and shy. "My mother is anything but. She practically screams and shrieks in public," Katelyn says, "and I get so humiliated I want to hide. Plus, she's always telling me to stop mumbling and speak up."

For Hillary, 14, the differences between her and her mother have even worse consequences. "My mother is a homebody. She's happy just blabbing on the phone to her friends once in a while. She doesn't understand why I want to be at my friend's house all the time." What makes Hillary feel bad, she says, is that "It seems like my mom thinks there's something wrong with me because I like to go out with my friends. When she was my age, she hung out with her mom." Once Hillary realized her desires were pretty normal, she spoke to a sympathetic aunt and then got the courage to broach the subject with her mom. "My mom actually thought I couldn't stand her," Hillary says, "but once she realized that I was just trying to have a social life, she seemed to relax."

This, too, is an important distinction. Be clear that your desire to do things differently from your mom is not an indirect way of showing you're angry or pushing her buttons. Then make sure your mom knows it, too. It's a whole lot easier for each of you to deal with the others' differences if you know they're genuine—and not intentional or personal.

We realize you could probably add about a dozen more issues to this list. We also realize there will surely be times when there'll be no terrific compromise in sight. No matter how much you discuss, negotiate, or agree to disagree, the differences between you and your mom will threaten to drive you both up a wall. What do you do then? Here are strategies that can alleviate painful differences between you and your mom:

Dear Carol: My older sister is 15 and won't stop spying on me. When I'm out, she goes through everything in my room-e-mails, cards, everything. I tried talking to her about it, but she said, "I have a life of my own. Why would I want to spy on yours?" It gets worse. She went through my underwear drawer and found some bras. Then she called her friends to tell them I was wearing a bra. Can't a girl have any privacy at all?—ENOUGH IS ENOUGH

Dear Enough: Sounds like she's threatened by the fact that her kid sister isn't as much of a kid anymore. Don't scream at her (though it may be tempting). Instead, tell her two things you like about her and that you feel hurt and betrayed when she goes through your stuff. Remind her that if there's something she wants to know, she can just ask you. Also if you can, confide in her at times. She may imagine that the only way into your life is to invade it. Point out that you respect her privacy (do you?). If all else fails, enlist the help of a parent.

1. See each other's point of view. Actually stop and think how you would feel if you saw things as your mom does. Let's say she's always getting upset about stuff lying around the house, but for you, the more clutter the better. Because you see the world so differently, not a day goes by without sparks (and clothes) flying. Try to think of something you yourself like neat and organized (like, say, your favorite accessories) and imagine how you'd react if someone scattered them around the house. It's perfectly okay to ask your mom to do the same when she's having trouble seeing your viewpoint. If you and your mom put yourselves in each other's places, you won't necessarily agree, but empathizing will put you in a better frame of mind to smooth your differences.

2. Let little things go. Getting riled up about every teensy-weensy difference of opinion, like who likes which style of napkin folding, will wear everybody out. Actually, most girls report feeling most panicky about the differences that show up in their mothers' fashion choices. Even the thought of being seen with a mother who perms her bangs, wears moccasins and purple jumpers—well, you can imagine. But who cares if her hot pink lipstick is vile? Try to remember that your mom's tacky vest or ugly hair clip does not reflect on your choices. Ignore the little stuff and make a stink only when it truly counts.

3. Appreciate your differences. Hard to imagine, huh? But it can work. Rather than each of you trying to "convert" the other, why not learn to make the most of differences? Well, let's start with just accepting differences. Suppose your mom is high-strung, always flying off the handle, while you're more laid back. Since it's unlikely that even your best, cleverest or sneakiest efforts will do a thing to change her, maybe you could learn to accept her instead. Just say to yourself, "It's okay, it's just mom's way." Anyway, there'll be plenty of personality differences between you and various friends, teachers and future roommates. By working things out with your mom, you'll learn to get along with all kinds of people.

4. Relish your differences. Consider this: What if it were a friend, rather than your mother, who suggested doing something pretty offbeat? You might still think it was weird, but you'd probably be a whole lot more open to the possibility. So just because it's your mom try not to immediately trash new experiences she offers. Sure, if your mom is gung-ho on your joining the church choir or a ham radio club and you're aghast, you can nix the idea. But if she's into bicycle races and you're into shopping sprees, what do you lose if you give her passion a try? And don't hesitate to ask her if she'll be open to your game plans, too. Instead of treating your differences as bones of contention, think of them as the spice of life.

Dear Carol: My dad ran away when I was a baby and I haven't seen him since. I keep wishing he would come back. I do have a stepfather but I wish I had a real father.—DAD LEFT

Dear Dad Left: I'm sorry your biological father has not been there for you. That is a big loss for him and you. While it's tempting to idolize your dad and dream about a reunion, he has a new life and hasn't been responsible for you for years. It's time to accept this and focus on the adults who care about you now. You say you wish you had a real father—but is your stepfather there for you? If so, *he* is a real father. Parenthood is about taking care of children, not just having children. Your feelings are natural, but being realistic about your past will help you heal and have a brighter future.

5. Find your commonalities. When all else fails, it may be comforting to know that aside from looks, personality, biorhythms, and hobbies, you and your mom do have something in common. Just what is it, though? It could be something small—like your love of singing silly songs in the car or watching lightning storms. Maybe you share things as basic—and important—as values. You both, for example, think women's rights, world peace, a clean environment, or protecting animals are key issues. Most likely, you also have in common something pretty helpful—an interest in getting along better with each other.

Mom Envy

When Your Mom's Too Cool or Not Cool Enough

Mom's red-and-blue plaid pants never embarrassed you before. You didn't used to cringe when she called you "precious" in front of friends or danced around shaking her thing to Richard Simmons' *Sweatin' to the Oldies* video. That was just Mom.

But suddenly, Mom's endearing little traits are grating on your every nerve. Your friends' moms are so much cooler. Well, listen closely because we're going to help ease your nerves, while keeping your relationship with Mom intact.

Take Jenny, 12, who used to be totally proud that her mom was so fashionable. She once loved clothes shopping with her mother, who had a flair for matching clothes with tons of funky accessories. But lately, seeing her mother so dressed up really bugs Jenny. The situation came to a head one day as she was standing in the school courtyard talking to her friends. When her mom came to pick her up and got out of the car, Jenny hated what her mother was wearing—pants that matched her blouse that went with her sweater, shoes, scarf and earrings. It was too much. "I was humiliated,"

Jenny says. "It wouldn't have been so bad, but I heard two guys from gym class laughing at her."

Similarly, Alice, 13, used to be proud that her mom was younger and prettier than her friends' moms. But now that Alice's mom dresses in the same clothes Alice and her friends wear, she feels ashamed of her. One day her mother came downstairs in a funky pair of jeans and beaded bracelets, in front of Alice's best friend. She wished she could tell her friend that her mom didn't usually dress like that but, in truth, she does. "At first, I didn't realize it," says Alice, "but whenever I thought she was trying to be cool, I found myself saying some pretty nasty and insulting things." Her mom became hurt and angry, and before they knew it, the two were arguing about all sorts of unrelated stuff.

It's pretty easy for hurt feelings to start arguments that get out of hand quickly. You don't want to tell Mom that she's embarrassing you, so you take it out on her in other ways. You say things that are really cruel or refuse to do the dishes. Of course, this makes things worse. The best way to handle the situation is to gather your courage and talk to her honestly about your embarrassment. If you express your true feelings and listen to her side, you should be able to work out ways to solve the problem.

You may want to talk to a friend before sitting down with your mom. For one thing, you'll get all the pent-up anger out of your system so you don't blow up at your mom later. You'll probably get sympathy from your pal, but you may even get a whole different viewpoint. For example, when Jenny complained to her friend Wendy about her mother's slick outfits, she was shocked by Wendy's reaction. "At least you have a mother who's with it," said Wendy. "My mother's still living in the '70s. She sews me these awful dresses and expects me to wear them to school. I don't want to be mean, but people would think I'm totally weird if I wore them." Jenny realized that maybe her situation wasn't so horrible after all.

When you do sit down to talk with your mom, try to say something positive first. That'll take the sting out of telling her that she embarrasses you. Say something like "Thanks for trying to fit in with me, but it bothers me when..." Tell her specifically what it is that embarrasses you. Saying "You always play stupid music" is insulting and will probably just make her angry. Instead try "It's embarrassing to me when you play your Sonny and Cher albums while my friends are over. Could you please wait until they're gone?"

Dear Carol: My parents are divorced, and I live with my dad. I see my mom every other weekend. I am happy the way I am living now, but my mom wants me to live at her house. She just finished school and has a job. I told her I don't want to live there, but she insists. My teacher even said I should live with my mom. I love my mom and like seeing her, but I am happy the way I am now.—TUG OF WAR

Dear Tug: Laws differ from state to state, but it seems to me that if your dad has custody and you're happy, things are settled. What caused your teacher to get involved? Does she distrust your dad? Ask if you're curious, but the point is: If you and your dad are content where you are, you don't have to move. Do, however, reassure your mom that you love her and like your living arrangement.

Always keep the discussion on track. Do not go off on the way she nags when you don't clean the dishes or finish your broccoli. That will only cause you guys to get sidetracked, making you both even more upset.

For Wendy, it was hard talking to her mother about the handmade clothes without hurting her feelings. Feeling trapped, she finally decided to speak to her guidance counselor, who gave her great advice: "I didn't tell my mother how awful or out-of-date the clothes are. I just said I appreciate her making them for me, but my tastes have changed and I want to experiment with different stuff. She didn't get mad

Image 13.1

at all. We even talked about ordering from some catalogs."

Once you tell her the problem, ask her if she'd like a cooling-off period to think about what you said, before trying to come up with solutions. Show your mom that you still like her—you just don't like something specific she's doing. Once you tell her what embarrasses you, don't go off and sulk or ignore her. Hug her. Now's the time to do something thoughtful. Also, cut her a break. You may need to remind her a few times to change her behavior—old habits die hard.

What if you gather your courage, wait until your mom seems relaxed and say all the "right" things, but she still goes ballistic? When Jenny told her mom she was embarrassed by her overly funky fashions and wished she'd dress a little more "normal," her mother exploded and told her to mind her own business. Jenny, hurt and surprised, yelled back, making things much worse. (Image 13.1)

"At first, I wished I'd never said anything," says Jenny. "But I'm glad I did. I now know that she might get angry, but she will eventually calm down. And then we can deal with the problem. I also learned to say 'Time out!' if she is yelling, which means 'I'm not going to stand here and listen to you scream at me.'" Just because you make your mom angry doesn't mean you're a bad person or that you necessarily did something wrong. Says Jenny, "I feel horrible when Mom and I get into a fight, but it's always worth it once we figure out what to do about it."

There's something else you should be prepared for. There are times when it isn't possible—or even appropriate—for your mom to do something differently just because it's embarrassing to you. It's okay to ask Mom to stop calling you "pumpkin" or telling you to clean up while friends are over. But there are some things you'll just have to deal with.

Let's go back to Alice. No matter how much Alice dreaded her mom's jeans and jewelry, she couldn't really expect her mother to stop wearing them. Just as girls want to choose their own outfits and be their own person, so do mothers. When Alice told her mom she didn't like her outfits, her mom basically said "too bad" because she really did like her clothes. Says Alice, "I knew we would never agree about it, but it's not going to change. So I guess I'll just have to live with it."

If talking face-to-face just seems too awkward or scary, try writing a note to your mom. Many girls find it easier to describe their feelings on a piece of paper, taking all the time they need. You can think through what you want to say. It might also be easier for your mom to understand your message if she can read it quietly in her own time. That way, she has a chance to think about her response without being put on the spot. Often, these notes between mothers and daughters can become a great way of communicating with each other.

Girls are most comfortable when their mothers aren't extreme—too cool or too uncool. They want friends to like their moms, but not too much. They want their moms to chat with pals, but not spend the afternoon hanging out with them.

Thirteen-year-old Hillary was tired of her mom spending so much time with her and her friends. Her excitement about an upcoming school ski trip was dampened by the thought of her mother sitting on the same bus as chaperone: "My mother is the type who wants to be one of the gang. It used to be great. But now when I have my friends over to the house, my mom is always around. I just want to have time with my friends—alone. I used to love it when she came along on field trips, but now I want someone else's mother to be the chaperone."

Fortunately, Hillary was able to explain how she felt so her mother didn't take her request as a personal rejection. "I told her the truth—that it was important to me to have some privacy with my friends," Hillary says.

Katie, 11, had the opposite problem. Katie's mom was at work or on the road a lot, and she wished her mother would hang out more with her and her friends. She felt bad going to her friends' houses all the time, but she wasn't allowed to invite her friends over when nobody was home. Says Katie, "Actually, my mom felt good when I told her I really wanted my friends to meet her. So we planned a sleepover one weekend when she wasn't traveling." They also decided Katie should invite friends over whenever her mother had the day off from work.

It's wonderful to enjoy and admire other people's moms. They all have their good and bad points. The truth is no mother is perfect—no birth mother, no stepmother, no adoptive mother and nobody else's either. Mothers can and do make mistakes, just like daughters. As one mother put it, "My daughter didn't come with an instruction manual."

One of the best things mothers and daughters can do is respect each other. That includes accepting each other's mistakes. Surefire ingredients for a great relationship include apologizing and quickly moving on afterwards.

Also, spend plenty of time doing fun stuff together. Spend the day window shopping, planting a flower garden, or going to a movie or for an afternoon hike. Set aside a regular, special time just for the two of you. You may want to go for breakfast on Saturday mornings or for dinner on Wednesday nights. During your time together, arrange to be alone, away from interruptions of siblings and the telephone. Not only will this time make your friendship stronger, it will also make it easier to start discussions if and when things bother you in the future.

Daddy's Little Girl?

Not!

Image 14.1

Every Father's Day you buy Dad something nice—a book or tie, give him a card signed with loads of love, then spend the day doing something fun with him.

But what about the rest of the year? Is your dad someone you can hang out with? Does he have any clue what's happening in your life? Let's face it—for many girls, it has become much easier to go to friends for advice. And if you can't talk to them, chances are you head to Mom (being a survivor of weird girl stuff herself). So where does that leave Dad?

For some, Dad is Mr. Disciplinarian—the one who lays down the law. Maybe he's the wallet holder, the one who rules the cash flow. Or maybe he's just the guy who says, "That's great, honey," before he buries his nose back into the paper. He has his job, his hobbies, and his pals.

A lot of girls have dads just like that. And they all want to know "How can I get closer with him?" It's not that most girls and their dads don't get along; it's just that after age ten or so, things sometimes take a turn for the distant. And if he wants a closer relationship with you, he'd have said something, right?

Not necessarily. Just as you may feel uncertain about your relationship, so does he. Don't forget, he has watched you choose to become closer to your friends. And he understands that you have more in common with Mom. But there's a good chance he feels left out.

What should you do about it? You can ignore it—but you'll be missing out on plenty. For one thing, Dad can introduce you to a whole new way of thinking. Men and women think and respond differently. (As one author puts it, men are from Mars, women are from Venus.) Whereas women tend to listen to others' problems and offer understanding and support, men tend to seek practical solutions to fix problems.

Dads can also explain the often confusing "male point of view." Who better to explain why the guys in your class do and say what they do than another male?

Last is this important fact: You are the product of him and your mom. Understanding your dad will help you better understand yourself.

So how do you start building a friendship? Here's a radical thought—tell him you want to. We're not saying it's a piece of cake. It takes courage to tell your dad you want to spend more time with him. It can be equally difficult to go to him with a problem for the first time. There's the risk that he might not act like you'd hoped. Sometimes he won't. But think how great it will be once you are able to gain each other's trust.

Here's what three girls did to get closer to their dads. All three started by admitting they wanted more from their dads than they were getting. Although none of them would say it was easy, they all feel the effort was worth their while.

WORK COMES FIRST

Eleven-year-old Molly looks a lot like her dad and has always been told she "has his eyes." The two used to spend a lot of time together. But something started bugging Molly this year. She played basketball in an intramural league, but her dad never came to any of her games, despite the fact that they were scheduled on late afternoons, evenings, and weekends. All the other kids' parents seemed to find time to watch.

What made it worse was knowing how much her dad loved watching basketball on TV. When Molly admitted to a teammate how much his absence disappointed her, the teammate suggested she talk to her dad. But how—and what if he didn't care?

After his no-shows at a few more games, Molly realized she would have to say something or end up really angry at him. So the day before a big game, Molly sat and watched basketball on TV with her dad. They did lots of cheering and pigging out on chips. And at the end of the game, Molly took a deep breath and decided to chance it.

"I asked him why he never came to my basketball games, since he obviously likes the sport so much," Molly says. "He told me it was because he has to work. So I told him the next game wasn't until 7:30P.M..., and he just said, 'We'll see.'" Although Molly could have left it at that, she decided to go the final step: "I told him it would really mean a lot to me if he showed up." He said he'd try, and Molly tried not to be too hopeful.

Happily, Molly's father did show up at the game to cheer her on. It wasn't picture perfect. "I made a few clumsy moves on the court," she says, "and I wanted to tell him I usually play better. But on the way home, he said I did well and gave me suggestions on playing my position. He doesn't go to every game now, but he goes to a lot more than he used to." Best of all, Molly is more comfortable telling her dad about personal stuff now that she knows he takes her feelings seriously.

STEPPING IN FOR MOM

Last year, Melinda, 14, was having a major friend problem. Jen, the friend, told a boy that Melinda was sometimes "so stuck up." When the boy went back and told Melinda, she was devastated. Worse, Melinda had no idea what to do.

Normally, she would have just talked to her mom. The two had always been close, and Melinda could tell her mother about almost anything. But there was one problem. Melinda's mother was away on business for a few days and Melinda didn't feel comfortable talking to her dad, who was always involved in his own activities. When she was younger, her dad was constantly taking her to restaurants, concerts, and other neat places. It seemed, however, he had less and less time for her these days. So why would he have time for her now? How could he even begin to understand or help her deal with her feelings?

Melinda sat and moped in her room, hoping her mom would call. But the longer she waited, the worse she felt. So she decided to brave it. It was scary, she says. She kept wondering what she'd do if her dad ignored her or said she should just wait until Mom gets home.

When her dad got home from work, Melinda asked if she could talk to him. It started off badly. "When I asked if he had a minute, he said, 'Let me unload my briefcase.' I couldn't believe it," Melinda says. "Once again, work was more important than me." But instead of walking away hurt, Melinda told him she really needed to speak with him right away. He looked surprised, but asked what was up.

"I told him everything that happened," Melinda says, "and I kept waiting for him to nod his head like Mom. She always handles problems right away." Her father, on the other hand, listened and then said she should give him an hour to think it over to come up with an idea. She went up to her room, disappointed.

"I really thought he was trying to blow me off," says Melinda. "I just about gave up. But he called me downstairs forty-five minutes later. He suggested I tell Jen how angry I was that she gossiped about me. He said I should, however, measure this one incident against all the good ones I'd had with Jen. We could definitely get through it. But the best thing he said was that guys aren't going to base friendships with me on what Jen says. I think that's what I needed to hear."

Melinda now goes to both parents when something is really bugging her. They always have different approaches, but both are usually helpful.

CHOOSING FAVORITES

Twelve-year-old Ellen likes her older sister Amy but couldn't stand that Amy got all her dad's attention. When Amy talked about school, Dad asked questions and joked around. He even went to all Amy's dance recitals. But when Ellen complained to her dad about always having to sit in the back seat of the car, he was annoyed with her for whining. Ellen explains, "I can't believe it now, but I actually counted the number of times in a week Amy got to sit in front with Dad and how many times I got to. It came out that she got to sit up front twice as much. I know it was dumb, but I was trying to prove that he was nicer to Amy."

Since scorekeeping didn't work, Ellen tried a new strategy. She tried to be as much like Amy as she could. She dressed like her, took dance class and talked about the same stuff Amy talked about. But soon Ellen realized she hated dance class, and wearing dresses. Amy constantly screamed at Ellen for being a "copy cat," and Ellen got no more positive attention from her dad than she started with.

"Finally, I got so mad that I went and talked with Dad," says Ellen. "I told him I felt like I was being ignored, and I could not be Amy. He looked surprised and said he didn't want me to be Amy. He told me to try activities I enjoy."

So Ellen followed his advice. She took up chess after school and got hooked on figuring out math problems. When Ellen discussed her hobbies during dinner, her dad asked questions about the problem-solving she was doing. He even asked if she would teach him to play chess. "He's pretty bad," Ellen confides, "but at least he's taking the time to learn. That's cool."

According to Ellen, she's also been spending a lot less time worrying about how much attention her dad gives Amy.

HOW WELL DO YOU KNOW DAD?

1. Where did your father grow up?

2. Did he go to college? Where?

3. Who were his best friends growing up?

4. Who are his best friends now?

5. What are his hobbies?

6. What's his favorite sport?

7. Does he like to read?

8. What does he do at his job all day?

9. What did he want to be when he was growing up?

10. How did he meet your mother?

To score, go sit with Dad and ask him for the answers. Whether or not your answers match, you're bound to find some interesting conversation starters.

As Ellen found out, it's a pretty bad idea to take on activities because you think it will please your dad (or anyone else, for that matter). You're much better off joining clubs that make you happy. Ellen's advice: "Trust me, you can't win your dad over through whining or trying to be someone you're not. If you want to spend more time with him, there's only one thing to do: Tell him."

One last point. After letting Dad know that you want him to take more of an interest in your life, return the favor. Ask him what activities he enjoys, and take part once in a while. Find out his likes, dislikes, talents and dreams. Asking him questions from the quiz on this page will get you headed in the right direction.

Fess Up to the Folks

Tips for Coming Clean to Your Parents

"Shoplifters will be prosecuted." The sign was glaring at Jessy from above her friend Tam's head in a dressing room. The same dressing room where Tam was stuffing a shirt into her backpack. "Come on," Tam said, shoving a pair of socks at her, "Take 'em." Jessy heard herself say okay, as she stuffed them in her pants. "Meet me outside!" Tam whispered. Her heart pounding, Jessy followed Tam through racks of clothes toward the door. The guard at the entrance looked right at them. Did he know? They kept walking. This was it. Act casual. Walking, walking....

"Excuse me," the guard said, blocking their path. "You have to come with me."

Busted! With the socks wedged between Jessy and her jeans, the security guard searched her backpack and found nothing. When they searched Tam's backpack, they found the stolen shirt. So who got in trouble? Just Tam. While she got to meet the mall police, Jessy was escorted out of the store. On her way to the bus stop, Jessy wondered what would happen to her friend. Will Tam tell her mom what really happened? More important, will Tam's mom call Jess's mom? Should she have confessed about the

Image 15.1

socks? Should she tell her mom everything when she gets home? Talk about a long bus ride!

And talk about a dilemma. If you've ever been in a situation where you've blatantly screwed up, you know how hard it is to make everything right again. Jessy made a major mistake and had to decide how to deal. Not easy. The obvious solution is to just confess and get the inevitable over with. Moms, dads and even psychologists will tell you that's the decision you ought to make.

Still, it's not hard to understand the back-and-forth panic you go through when there's a fifty-fifty chance you might not get ratted out. That little devil on your shoulder sometimes tells you to play the odds by taking the easy way out (crossing your piggies and hoping you don't get caught).

Of course, there's the other fifty percent chance Mom's going to get the dreaded call, and you'll be in double trouble for not spilling the beans yourself.

Our advice: Turn yourself in. Yeah, we know you want to hear about a magic potion to make the whole thing just go away, but we just don't have that recipe. We can, however, tell you how to make the task of telling your folks a bit easier. If you're in a dilemma where you need to tell Mom or Dad about a bummer situation—or even if you just want to buff up on your parent strategies for the future—here are five basic tips to remember.

1. Expect to be nervous. Knowing you need to confess when a bad scene has gone down is just the beginning. We admit the actual act of choking up a confession is harder than French-braiding your hair with two broken arms. The best plan of action? Don't pretend it's not a bad situation. It is.

Your mom and dad usually know when you're hiding something or when something is bugging you. The chances that they won't read your bad vibes are pretty slim. But your parents probably aren't going to be as concerned with *how* you tell them, just as long as you *do* tell them and own up to your mistakes. So when you're thinking about how to announce the messy details of your latest (gulp!) screw-up, expect a band of butterflies to flutter around. Throw in sweaty palms, pounding heart, throbbing head, and stuttering voice, and you have yourself a ticket to Confession City. (Image 15.1)

2. Don't predict the reaction. You're sure fessing up is going to cause a reaction. With that confession just minutes away, you have important things on your mind: Exactly what will that reaction be? Will they be high-voltage ballistic, mildly angry, or low-level peeved? The answer: flubbaglup! Meaning: Don't bother trying to figure this one out! Your parents' behavior is not predictable.

No matter if you're exiled to your room until your eighteenth birthday or simply forbidden to watch Simpsons reruns (which you've seen a million times anyway), the punishment does not always match the deed. Rumor has it moms and dads own a parenting manual to consult when you commit a kid crime. But parents only wish they had it so easy.

3. Get straight to the point. Ever have a friend rush up after class to tell you how crushed she is over getting a C in history? But before she actually gets to the C part, she has to explain how the teacher hates her, how the test wasn't fair, how her head was throbbing, blah, blah, blah. The point is she got a bad grade. Period. When too many details tie up the story, the truth gets confused in all the drivel.

That's why this is the most crucial part of the strategy. When it comes to stuff that's going to raise eyebrows of disapproval, there's only one plan: Spit it out! Otherwise, parents will get lost (and probably ticked) in the build-up. Start with these words: "Mom and Dad, I have something important to tell you." Then tell them the climax of the story first! No speeches about events (and no philosophies on grounding).

4. Don't blame others. You dropped the bomb. Now what? There you are, sitting across the kitchen table from the let-down faces of the folks. It's 7 P.M., and you have no idea what's coming next.

Did someone say "lecture?" Lec-ture. Say it to yourself because that's what you're likely to get once you've admitted your mistake. Though you've fessed up, you still have to deal with the consequences of your mess up. (Remember? That's why you're here.) Sorry, but if you expect your parents to pat you on the head like the family retriever and tell you thanks for owning up, you're living a fantasy.

Now that you've gotten straight to the point and confessed, it's time for the parents' verdict (commonly called "The Talk"). But don't fret. The key to getting through The Talk is to actually listen to what your parents have to say and answer third-degree questions directly. Now is when they'll want those details (the parts we told you to tuck away until you got the real goods out in the open).

Jessy's mom wanted to know what happened in the dressing room. "I told her Tam made me take the socks," remembers Jessy, "but for some reason, that made her more upset." Jessy's mom was angry because Jessy wasn't owning up to what she did. How does a girl own up? Say you're sorry. When you fess and then apologize for what you've done, you show you take responsibility for your actions.

Even though that may sound like a cliché to roll your eyes at, the truth is, accepting responsibility is what will keep the steam from shooting out of an angry parent's ears. Don't blame the other kids who were involved. If you own up to your actions by saying you're sorry, you trumpet to mom and dad that you didn't mean to do wrong. It's a gesture that may also, by the way, lessen restriction time and change chore lists from heavy-duty overhauling to light dusting. Think about it.

5. Promise it won't happen again. When we make mistakes, we're supposed to learn something. That's why certain promises have to be made. A promise that you won't make the same mistake twice puts a big Band-Aid on the situation and helps rebuild that trust. You can repair the trust-injury by promising a ten-foot pole between you and all future dabbles in whatever trouble (future or right now) you may attract. Then you have to keep that promise. And trust us, you can do it.

The Big "D"

How to Cope When Your Folks Split

Image 16.1

Sure, you know people get divorced. Until recently, however, it was only other kids' parents. Now maybe you've joined the ranks of 1.5 million kids whose parents divorce every year. Maybe you felt numb when you first heard; then came sadness, confusion, anger, fear. Face it, there are loads of changes to get used to—having two homes, juggling a different schedule, and remembering in whose house you left your math homework. As if that weren't bad enough....

Perhaps the biggest challenge of all is when parents are waging battle against each other. In this giant tug-of-war, you're smack in the center, feeling pulled apart. But the most important thing to remember is that your parents are splitting from each other, not from you.

So no matter what happens between them, your goal is to have the best relationship you can with your mother, as well as the best relationship you can with your father. Separate relationships. How? Stay out of whatever conflicts arise between your parents. It's almost never advisable to take sides. We can't say this strongly enough. No good will come out of getting involved. None, zip, nada. Thankfully, there are ways to stay neutral ... and stay sane.

OPEN WARFARE

In a perfect world, adults would never argue. In a semi-perfect world, they would argue in private. Kids would be spared the raised voices, icy tones, and harsh words that spill in the heat of anger. Although many parents try to protect kids from conflicts, sometimes their emotions get the best of them, particularly during the stress of separation or divorce. As a result, kids witness fights they wish they'd never seen. Katie, 12, went through this for two years before her parents finally divorced. "As soon as I heard them yelling," she says, "I'd go in my room, get under my covers and put my Walkman on real loud."

It's even tougher when parents openly express hostility about each other to their kids. "All my mom and dad did was badmouth each other," says Minnie, 12. "As soon as they got me alone, they'd each say hateful things about each other. I didn't know what to do." It's hard to hear a parent you love speak badly about the other. Although your first instinct may be to defend the parent who's not there, that tactic backfired on 14-year-old Martha. "I ended up getting into fights with each parent about the other one." Ellen, 13, perhaps has the best suggestion: "I listen, but don't say a word."

If a parent doesn't pick up the silent message that you're uncomfortable hearing your other parent get bashed, you might have to speak up. Rather than scolding, say what you feel: "It's awful to hear bad things about Dad," or "I know you're angry, but it hurts when you say you hate Mom," or "I love you both, so please leave me out of it." Ideally, your parents will keep their problems with each other separate from you.

IF LOOKS COULD KILL

Sometimes disapproval is expressed subtly—not with mean words or flying objects, but with a certain sigh, an eye-roll, or raised eyebrow whenever the other parent's name comes up. Says Katherine, 14, "My parents would never come out and say anything, but every time I talk about my father, my mother gets a weird look on her face. It makes me wonder what I've done wrong."

Ignoring the signals of hidden anger won't make them go away, so you might want to mention that they make you uncomfortable. Many parents don't realize their body language screams hostility. And for a while, you may want to put a lid on gushing to your mom about the awesome time you had with your dad. Or skip mentioning your mom's cool new friend to your dad.

THE BLAME GAME

When it's clear one parent wanted the divorce and the other didn't, it's harder to avoid taking sides. You and one parent want to be a family again; the other parent is to blame for all the misery!

Becky, 14, confides, "My mom found someone else and didn't want to be married to my dad anymore. He was devastated. I felt sorry for him—and my-self—and blamed her. It was years before I realized it wasn't that simple." Even when you think you know what's going on, you may not. Taking sides may help you express your anger, but placing blame won't accomplish much. In fact, you could wreck a close, healthy relationship with each par-ent.

WHAT'S IN IT FOR ME?

Girls think they're being neutral, but sometimes—maybe without realizing it—they manipulate situations to their advantage. Say you and your dad are fighting about privileges. You think he's setting unreasonable rules. Mom has her own beef with him. So when she complains, you don't zip your lip about your own issues with Dad. You fuel the fires of her anger. Now she's in complete sympathy with you about Dad's stubbornness and pressures him to lighten up. Good work? It may seem so. You've gone to more parties and finagled extra phone time, but you've gotten nowhere in the process of working out stuff with your dad. Having a relationship with him where you can negotiate rules is far more important in the long run than a short term victory.

TELL ME ABOUT IT

Parents often ask girls for info about the other parent. It can be as innocent as "Did your father get the photo albums I sent him?" or as probing as "Is your mom getting serious with that man?". When parents are in conflict, communication between them might be at a standstill. So they may use these questions as easy ways to find out stuff they're curious about.

But when girls feel parents are pumping them for information, they're understandably uneasy. "When my dad asked me what time my mom gets home at night, and if we were ever left alone," says Sara, 12, "I was worried that whatever I say might be used against her." Andrea, 11, agrees. "I never know what to say. If I answer, I wonder if I'm telling on the other parent."

This can be tricky for parents too. One divorced father confessed, "I'm so tempted to ask my children things about their mother. I actually have to stop myself because I know it's not right."

If your parent doesn't realize this is a problem for you, you may have to say, "Why don't you ask Mom?" or "I'd feel better if you could ask Dad that question." That way, you're wiggling out of the middle without being cagey or rude.

But if you're being placed in a dangerous situation—or truly being neglected or mistreated—do not keep quiet, even if telling someone might make your parents' conflict worse. Your safety comes first. If you'd rather not tell the other parent, speak to a trusted relative, teacher, guidance counselor, friend of the family, doctor, or religious leader.

HE SAID, SHE SAID

"At first I thought, 'What's the big deal?'" says Anna, 12. "My mom asked me to tell my dad about my teacher conference, but he flipped out. He started yelling about how come he wasn't told before, why was it scheduled in the middle of the workday, blah, blah, blah. He just went off on my mom."

Emily, 12, confides, "My father asked me to tell my mom that he needed to switch weekends with her. I didn't want to, but what could I say? So when I got home and told her, she got all quiet and went to her room. It wasn't my fault!"

It may seem like a perfectly harmless request: "Tell your mother I'll take you to school in the morning," or "Ask your father about that child support check." But carrying messages back and forth is a surefire way to get yourself smack in the middle—even if you thought there was no conflict. To keep out of the crossfire, suggest that parents leave messages on each other's office answering machines or send e-mail. That way, they can avoid face-to-face or phone confrontations, and you can avoid being the messenger.

OH, THERE'S MORE?

When parents split up, they lose a lot too. So it's only natural they might try to hold on to what they value most—you. Sometimes parents try to show how much they love their kids by giving them lots of toys, clothes, jewelry, whatever. To make up for the hurt of a divorce, other parents try to have fun every minute they spend with their children. Constant outings, movies or zoo trips, anything to entertain. "I can't believe I'm saying this," says Sally, 11, "but it gets to be a bit much. He never did this when they were married."

For Fran, 12, it came down to a competition. "It's like they're trying to outdo each other." It's bad enough when parents have equal resources. But often, one parent doesn't have as comfortable a lifestyle after a divorce. Evi, 13, found the gap painful. "My dad bought this great house and got me the horse I always wanted. He gives me anything I ask for. Meanwhile, Mom and I live in a tiny condo, and she can barely afford everyday stuff."

It's important to keep material things in perspective. It's fun to visit great places and get gifts, but if it feels like parents are competing for your love, it's time to say, "Time out!" Nobody likes to be fought over. When you're in the middle, you don't come out a winner. Yes, you might have your own horse, a box full of movie stubs, or enough nail polish to get you through 2010—but your relationships with both parents should be based on genuine caring, honesty, and affection.

Sometimes, you might have to point out to a parent that you don't expect—or even want—him or her to keep pouring money out for you. Molly, 14, says, "I was torn between enjoying all these great clothes my dad bought me and feeling bad because that was all we talked about. Finally, one night I blurted out, 'Dad, instead of going shopping this weekend, could we just go have lunch?' He seemed uncomfortable at first, and it seemed strange, but it was a start."

Toby, 10, spoke to her dad after realizing she was exhausted after weekends with him. "We were always running around—fun stuff—but it was too much. I told him I really wanted to just hang out with him sometimes, maybe play a game. I think he may have even been a little relieved."

Divorce or no divorce, if a parent unselfishly gives love and time, offers patience and a sympathetic ear, he or she is giving the ultimate gifts.

CUSTODY BATTLES

It's one thing for parents to disagree about where you'll spend a weekend or holiday, but quite another when they wage war over whose house you live in. Nearly everyone agrees when it comes to divorce that custody battles are the worst nightmare. Girls vary, however, on how much input they want in the decision that will transform their lives. "I don't want to have to choose who to live with," Ariel, 10, says directly. "But what if they make me?"

Dear Carol: My parents are divorced. My dad moved away to a different state. My mom won't let me spend the summer with my dad, but I want to.—MISSING MY FATHER

Dear Missing: I'm sorry you're going through a rough time. Can you ask your mom why she doesn't want to let you go all summer? Is it because she'll miss you or because she's mad at your dad or maybe doesn't trust him to take good care of you? Who has custody during the summer? If you can find out these answers, it will help you decide what to do. Explain to your mother that you miss your dad. Reassure her that you love her tons and will call and write her letters and send email and that you'll be back before she knows it. If there's a grandmother or aunt whom you trust, perhaps you can ask for advice or help from her, too. It's important to be sensitive to your mom's feelings, but it's also important to stay close to both of your parents, if possible.

Susannah, 14, feels differently. "I love both my parents," she says, "but I get along better with my mom. I'm more like her than my dad, so living with him would be uncomfortable."

What should girls do if they have a preference? Can they say their piece without offending either parent?

What are their rights? Although rules vary according to what state you live in, most laws say children are entitled to be appointed an adult representative (a guardian or attorney) by the court, who represents their best interests in the custody process. So, if you wish, you should have a chance to make your preferences known.

Your feelings, we admit, will be harder to deal with. There's no getting around it. Girls feel worried, angry, frustrated—even devastated—when parents fight over them. These feelings are perfectly normal and, hopefully, temporary. But it's an awful position to be in. Whatever you do, don't keep your feelings to yourself. This is the time to confide in trustworthy, neutral adults like school counselors, teachers and religious leaders. They may not be able to sway the process, but their caring and support can definitely help ease the pain and anxiety of this stressful situation.

The best thing you can do is take care of yourself. Where there's parent conflict and separation, there's hurt. Even though it was not your decision for parents to split, you have to accept what you can't change and find happiness in new ways. Though painful, a divorce doesn't have to destroy anyone's life. And, believe it or not, you can influence much of what happens after a divorce. How well you come through this process and get on with your life depends on your parents, of course, but also on your outlook, how much you deal with your feelings and how you handle situations that pop up. You can start by doing a lot of thinking about what's best for you. Here are some tips on how you can continue to take care of yourself by not getting caught in the middle:

1. Accept divorce as a permanent reality. In hoping that their parents will get back together, many girls are desperate to "help." The thinking goes "If only Mom realized what a great guy he is, she'd give Dad another chance," or "If Dad understood Mom's feelings, he'd come back." Sadly, nothing good ever happens when girls dive into the conflict. When their efforts fail, they often feel guilty and blame themselves. As hard as it is to accept, girls must realize they aren't responsible for fixing parents' problems. It's up to parents to work it out—or not.

2. Avoid conflict as much as possible. The fewer arguments you see or hear, the less you'll be drawn into the clash between your parents. If you find certain routines usually cause major scenes, such as when your dad brings you home after a weekend or when your mom drops you off, think about how to get around them. Consider staying outside until parents finish "talking." Call a friend, play loud music, go for a walk, cuddle a pet, or take a bike ride.

3. Make your life easier. When there's tension so thick you can practically touch it, special occasions can turn ugly. Think of how you can work things out to minimize weird vibes. You may have to celebrate your birthday and religious holidays twice. (This could have advantages.) There may be a way for one parent to visit camp one day, the other parent the next. Or split a school visiting day in half. Teachers usually are willing to have separate conferences if parents can't or won't go together. By speaking of your own discomfort and wish to keep peace, you avoid blaming either parent and let them know they're valued.

4. Monitor your own life. As you remove yourself from your parents' conflict, you'll be better able to pursue normal routines, activities, and friendships. But make sure you're not taking your feelings about the divorce out on others. For example, if you're suddenly mouthing off to teachers, getting in trouble or going ballistic on friends, this may be a sign your anger isn't resolved or being channeled well. It may take a while to feel like your old self, so give yourself a break. Be sure you're taking every chance to care about others and have them care about you. Enjoying healthy relationships is an important way of moving on after a divorce.

5. Feel the feelings. Divorce is hurtful—no doubt about it. It's tempting to avoid facing feelings. Some girls pretend they don't exist: "Oh, I could care less about the divorce." Others use alcohol or drugs to dull the pain, and some get so busy they don't have time to think. But if you don't deal with the feelings—that is, allow yourself to feel them, no matter how painful—you can't move on. You've experienced a huge loss, which can cause sadness, anger, worry, and confusion.

Don't let yourself suffer needlessly. Talking about what you're going through, confiding in special friends and caring, trusted adults, is a must. Sharing your feelings isn't betraying family business. Counselors, religious leaders, relatives, and friends' parents can keep discussions private. Support groups especially for kids whose parents are divorced are another resource.

In thinking about your future, post-divorce, here's our wish list:

- You will continue to have separate, healthy relationships with both your parents.

- They will put aside their differences enough to parent you together wisely.

- Parents will be supportive of your feelings.

- You'll still get to be a kid.

- You will stop blaming yourself for causing or not preventing the divorce. It had nothing to do with you.

- You will have loving relationships in years to come.

- You will forgive your parents.

Dear Carol: Lately, I've been feeling left out of my dad's life. Since he got a new girlfriend, I feel like she and I have to compete for his attention.—NEEDS ATTENTION TOO

Dear Needs: I wish I could write to your dad and not just to you. Since your father can't read your mind, you'll have to tell him how you feel. Don't say "You pay more attention to her than me." Instead try "Dad, I miss you. I don't see you often enough, so when we do get together it means a lot to me if we can do something, just us. What do you think?" I hope he realizes he's lucky to have a daughter who loves him. If all else fails, leave this book open on the desk with a Post-it that says, "I confess—I sometimes feel that way."

Wedding Bell Blues

What to Do When Parents Tie the Knot ... Again!

"If anyone is against this union, speak now or forever hold your peace." When Cindy, 13, heard the minister make this announcement she thought, "That's it!" Why hadn't she considered it before? All she would have to do was yell, "Stop! Hold everything. I am against this union!"

For an agonizing moment, Cindy tried to summon the nerve to do it. But she was living that nightmare where you're trying to scream and no sound comes out. "I realized at that moment that my dad was going to marry Monica no matter how I felt, and there wasn't a darn thing I could do about it."

Wait—weddings are supposed to be happy occasions, right? Well, Cindy was definitely experiencing a lot of emotions, but happy wasn't one of them. Anger, resentment, betrayal, and jealousy were just a few. Not to mention she felt a tinge of guilt for even having those feelings. But experiencing such emotions is perfectly normal because watching a parent remarry—even if you adore the soon-to-be-stepparent —can be an excruciating event in a girl's life.

There are ways, however, to make the new situation tolerable. Bear in mind, though, that things may not get better overnight—or even in a few weeks or months. It takes time to adjust.

ACCEPTING CHANGE

Getting used to the idea of a parent remarrying can be frustrating, but it does no good to sit around and mope about it. Cindy had an especially hard time shaking her negative attitude because she was just getting over the sting of her mom and dad being divorced. She wanted her parents to live out the happy fairy tale—married and in love forever. When they announced they were splitting up, it rocked Cindy's world. And now that her dad had a new wife, that ruined any chance of her parents reuniting.

Brianna, 12, had no hopes of her parents getting back together because her dad died when she was six. But when her mom got married to Rick, Brianna couldn't help feeling uneasy—even though "he's a great guy." It had been just Brianna and her mom for so long that she couldn't imagine it any other way. "You and I are a team," her mom always said. Now, a whole new player had been recruited. And even though he passed "tryouts," Brianna couldn't help feeling like she was being benched: "I liked Rick, but I couldn't help thinking he was trying to split us up." (Image 17.1)

Image 17.1

It's normal to feel overwhelmed. But, unfortunately, there are some things in life you have no control over—like when a parent decides to tie the knot. Cindy couldn't stop her parents' divorce, and Brianna can never bring her real dad back. Changes happen all the time in life, and the best thing you can do is try to change with it. "Once I accepted that I couldn't end the marriage," says

Cindy, "it really did take the edge off of my bad feelings."

SHARING

Many kids say the hardest part about being in a stepfamily is having to share a parent. Because Cindy's stepmom has two daughters, she has to share her dad with Monica, his new wife, and two stepsisters. "I was enjoying the special time my dad and I spent together on weekend visits," says Cindy. "And now, while I get only weekends with him, they get to live with him all week long. Like that's really fair!" And who could blame her for feeling that way? If you miss spending time with a parent, you should say so. After about two months of gritting her teeth over it, Cindy decided to sit down with her dad and chat.

She explained that she really missed the alone time she used to have with him. Her dad was cool about it, and they worked out an arrangement where every other weekend he and Cindy would do something together for at least an hour—just the two of them. They'd go for walks, get ice cream, whatever. Just so they had special time together.

But for some kids, like Jesse, 10, a parent might not be willing to spend one-on-one time. When Jesse, who has two stepbrothers, tried to talk to her dad, he said, "I have four children now, and I won't give special treatment to just one." Jesse was bummed, but she accepted it as one of those things that she just can't change. She takes solace knowing her dad really does love her. She also knows he's just trying to be fair to the other kids.

HOUSE RULES

A new stepparent sometimes comes with a roster of new rules and regulations—from seating arrangements at the dinner table to having the towels folded a specific way. For Brianna, the new rules were about curfews. Her mom used to let her go to Skateland every Friday night until midnight. That was her favorite part of the week, and half the kids from her grade went. "Well, Rick freaked out," she explains. "He changed my curfew to 11P.M.—and Mom let him!"

The new rules were an equal surprise to Cindy. When her dad first moved out and got his own place, it was pretty cool because things were so laid back: "I could put my feet on the table and eat Snickers bars for breakfast. I swear, I think I could have stuck wads of gum under the furniture and my dad wouldn't have cared." Not anymore! Cindy's stepmom is like Martha Stewart and expects everyone to help keep the house spotless. "Even Mom isn't this tidy," says Cindy.

It's hard adjusting to new rules, especially when things have been a certain way for so long. However—unless you think a specific rule is terribly unreasonable—you just have to deal. Rules can be particularly confusing when you live in two homes with two different sets of laws. If this is the case, write down the rules of each house and post them in plain sight.

ALL IN THE FAMILY

Dividing bathroom time with virtual strangers can be pretty unpleasant. Suddenly, your shampoo bottle is half empty or replaced by a stepsister's shaving gel. Even worse is being forced to share a bedroom.

On weekends with her dad, Cindy has to share a room with her oldest stepsister Samantha because they're about the same age. (Five-year-old Stephanie gets her own room. Go figure!) "I was an only child before Dad married Monica," she says, "so I always had my own room. It was weird to be sleeping in the same room and sharing drawer space with a girl I hardly knew. Not to mention that I thought she was a complete dork."

But Cindy decided to at least try to get along with Samantha. "Once I gave her a chance, I realized she's not so geeky. Honestly, I would probably never choose her as a friend, but we were thrown together so we make the best of it."

As for five-year-old Stephanie, Cindy thought, "What's wrong with me? Here's this cute little kid who's supposed to be my sister, so how come I don't feel like I love her?" Cindy soon figured out she doesn't have to love her stepfamily. Love is something that grows—it doesn't just happen because of some marriage certificate. You might never love (or even like) your stepkin like you do other relatives. Then again, maybe one day you will. Either way, it's okay. The important thing is to do your best to get along.

SOMETHING TO TALK ABOUT

If you're trying really hard to get along with members of your stepfamily but still having trouble, find someone to talk to. While it feels good to vent to a bud, you need someone who can offer trusted, helpful advice.

Lucky for Brianna, she was able to approach Rick when she was feeling angry or scared. But remember Jesse? She had a super hard time getting along with her stepmom. "She was mean," says Jesse. "She just waltzed in and took over. It seemed like Dad was totally brainwashed by her. He even stopped paying as much child support, and Mom was so stressed." Her mom being upset was rubbing off on Jesse, and her stomach was in knots.

"Things were spinning out of whack, so I knew I had to talk to someone," she explains. That's when Jesse went to see her school counselor. The counselor helped Jesse a lot and referred her to a support group with other kids from stepfamilies. They got together once a week, talked about things that bothered them, and helped each other deal: "That's where I learned all about accepting change and how to share and stuff."

Jesse found out that child support shouldn't concern her: "My counselor explained that it's an adult issue and it wasn't fair for Mom to burden me with it—though she didn't mean to hurt me."

She also learned an important lesson in communicating. If you plan to talk to a parent about something that's bothering you, use "I feel" sentences, such as "I feel hurt," or "I feel left out." Sentences that start with the phrases "You always..." or "You never..." make people feel they have to defend themselves instead of solving the problem. "I feel" sentences keep things in perspective and help others put themselves in your position.

For example, instead of "You always treat the other kids better," try "I feel that I'm not being treated fairly." When Jesse talked without blaming, her stepmom was able to better understand what was bugging her.

OH, THE GUILT

A lot of girls build an instant wall between themselves and a new stepparent. Jesse admits she was afraid to be nice to her stepmom because she felt guilty. Why guilty for trying to be nice of all things? Because she felt like she was betraying her mother if she started to care about her stepmom—especially since her mom didn't like her dad's new wife.

As much as Brianna liked Rick from the very start, she too went through tremendous guilt: "I felt like I was trashing the memory of my real dad. I didn't want to feel like I'd replaced him."

It's all right, even healthy, to have a good relationship with your stepparent. It takes nothing away from your feelings for your other parent. But what if you sense your parent, like Jesse's mom, feels threatened by this closeness? Jesse finds it works best to avoid blabbing on and on to her mom about her stepmom.

TIME OUT

If you're having a bad day, fighting with the stepbrother over the Game Boy or something, distance yourself for a while. Go for a walk, read a book, call a friend. Everybody needs and deserves private time. Because Cindy has to share her room, she had a hard time finding her own space at first: "If I went in the kitchen, there was my stepmom. If I went in the family room, there was little Steph. I felt smothered." So Cindy found herself a little spot in the basement where she goes just to chill and write in her diary.

She reminds herself of her role in keeping the peace. "Sometimes I think it's unfair that I have to make an effort for a situation I didn't choose, but it's okay."

The Evil Stepmother

Fact or Fiction?

Your parents divorce, and suddenly your picture-perfect family isn't so perfect anymore. It takes time, but most girls do get used to their parents leading new and separate lives. What might take more getting used to is their new and separate loves. While getting a new "mom" or "dad" can be equally daunting, it seems stepmothers present unique challenges. We can credit some of that dread to fairy tales. We all know what happened to Cinderella and Snow White. While we don't know any girls who spend their post-stepmom days scrubbing floors, wearing rags or eating poisoned apples, many say having a new "mom" brings on complicated questions and feelings.

Though Callie, 12, liked her stepmom-to-be well enough, the big announcement left her cold. "I knew I should feel happy for them—it's not that I didn't like her—but all I felt was hurt. My school counselor helped me realize how hard my parents' breakup was on me. She also pointed out that while I rationally knew my parents would never get back together, it took hearing Dad's big news to know in my heart that our family was really over."

Callie's feelings aren't that unusual. No matter how much you wish or pray or watch *The Parent Trap,* hearing that one parent is getting remarried forces you to accept that your family will never be the same again. But you can survive this final chapter of your parents' breakup ... and survive the first chapter of having a new family member.

FIRST REACTIONS

Sometimes, dealing with your feelings—good or bad—isn't the hard part. What's difficult is being told those feelings are wrong. It doesn't help when everyone tries to paint a cheerful picture. Just ask Susan, 12, who admits: "My aunts kept telling me how great having a stepmom is, but it didn't feel great to me."

Christina, 16, had the opposite experience when her father remarried. In the same way Susan felt pressured to be psyched about gaining a new stepmother, Christina was made to feel bad about being open to the idea. "My sister acted like I had stabbed her in the back, but I couldn't help liking my stepmom," she says.

Whatever your feelings about hearing your family portrait will be repainted, they are yours and yours alone. People can feed you opinions to chew on, but it's your decision to swallow them or spit them out.

Remember, nobody can (or should) ever try to force you to feel a certain way. As time passes, you may change your views, but in the meantime it's perfectly okay to say to others, "Give me some time to get used to all this" or "I see what you mean, but that's not how I feel right now." Likewise, you should give other people, like sisters and brothers, room to have their own feelings. No fair asking, "How could you possibly like her?" or "Why don't you try harder?"

"IT'S ALL HER FAULT."

When telling the kids about a divorce, most parents present a united front and stay away from issues of blame. It goes without saying that you should not feel responsible for the breakup. But when a girl-friend appears soon after a divorce, it's hard for girls not to point a finger her way.

Right after Heidi's parents called it quits, her father married his co-worker Stacey. "I hated her," Heidi, 14, confesses. "I thought if she had just stayed away from my dad at work, my parents would still be married and we'd all be happy." Heidi is the first to admit her fury made life pretty uncomfortable for everyone. When she finally struck up a conversation with her mother about the situation, Heidi says, "She told me I shouldn't blame Stacey, since both she and my dad had a lot of problems in the marriage."

If one of your parents immediately takes up with someone new, don't jump to conclusions (as hard as that might be). The changes in your family may seem sudden, but your parents have probably been adjusting for a while. It would be great if they had been happy together, but the best thing you can do is understand their wanting happiness and accept that a new person brings that into their life.

TWO'S NO LONGER COMPANY

Diana, 13, believes her stepmother has driven a wedge between her and her dad: "She makes my dad do so much stuff after work that he has no time for me." It's understandable if you're frustrated and upset about not getting as much alone time with your dad. But instead of taking it out on the family, your best bet is to pull your dad aside and talk to him. ("I miss our early breakfasts, just the two of us.") Then ask directly for what you'd like. ("Can we spend a little time alone together?")

Although it's unlikely things will go back to the way they were BSM (before stepmom), your dad might be happy to arrange some special time for the two of you. If your dad has trouble carving out time, don't lose hope and definitely don't blame yourself. The family changes affect him too, and he's probably having difficulties balancing it all. If he seems pulled in 200 new directions, give him a little time to adjust. Then try again. If he just can't seem to fit in some special time, accept that visits with him now include your stepmom and make the best of it.

SHE DRIVES ME CRAZY!

Image 18.1

Nobody's perfect, and that includes your stepmother. You'll undoubtedly find things about her that drive you batty. Maybe she'll talk too loud, expect too much from you, give too much input on your fashion choices, feed your dog the wrong way. But the two most frequent complaints girls give about stepmothers are "She tries too hard" or "She doesn't try hard enough." (Image 18.1)

Some girls resent overzealous stepmothers who try too quickly to get close or act like a parent. Amy, 10, believes that as soon as her stepmother met her, she "lost no time in stepping right in and telling me what to do and not do. I hate that. She's not my mother." That's true, she's not your mom. But she is an adult and she has probably been entrusted to take care of you, just like a teacher or an aunt.

Try to separate your anger over her presence from your anger at her barking orders. No one likes being told what to do, but we all make an effort at school and with family. If she is a 24/7 drill sergeant, you may need to bring in a trusted adult to help you and your stepmother communicate more effectively. But if she's just trying to keep things running smoothly, try cutting her a little slack.

Debbie, 13, complains that her stepmother acts too familiar, "like she's known me my whole life. She drops my friends' names as if she's known them forever!" Amanda, 14, whose father just got engaged, says of her future stepmother, "The lady acts like she's my best friend. If she plops down on my bed one more time, I am going to scream!" You may have to point out to your stepmother (gently, of course) that you need more time to feel close to her. It's better than flinching every time she puts an arm around you or plants a fat smooch on your cheek.

At the other extreme are girls who feel their stepmothers don't put enough effort into having a relationship with them, ignoring them or behaving as if they wish the girls weren't around.

Mindy, 13, says, "My stepmother acts all weird around me, like I'm an alien." Patty, 10, believes her stepmother can't stand her, since "she hardly ever talks to me, and whenever I say something to her, she acts like it was just stupid."

If you're feeling awkward around your stepmom, remember that she may be feeling just as anxious as you. She may want to get to know you but is afraid to push things or seem too eager. Perhaps she's never had a daughter or children of her own. Maybe she's not used to being around a girl your age.

And if you know that you might be doing something to make your stepmother feel bad—like the daggers you keep shooting her way, the sighs and snippy remarks, the eye-rolling—think about how it's impacting you and your family. It's hard for everyone to get along when one person is actively pushing others away. It may take time and even some counseling, but you need to try to find a way to at least have some family peace.

CHANGING FOR THE BETTER

You don't have to look for four-leaf clovers, throw pennies in a well, or snap turkey bones in half to improve your stepmother situation. Nor do you have to wait for Dad to clue in that you and she are not exactly tossing rose petals at each other. Instead, take matters into your own hands.

Start by being friendly and trying to get to know her, just as you would a new girl in school. Ask her to do something, just the two of you, like go for ice cream, play a video game, or take an afternoon hike. If you're not sure what to talk about, bring up things you have in common (other than your dad, that is), such as movies, books or sports. Ask about her job, her family or where she used to live. If none of this works and you still feel she is shunning you, bolster your courage and ask, "Could we try to get to know each other better?" or, if necessary, "Is there a reason you ignore me?"

Some problems with stepmothers, however, are too hard for girls to figure out—much less solve. Brenda, 13, found herself feeling bad because "nothing I try with my stepmother works. She took over our whole life along with our whole house. She even turned my old playroom into her personal home office. It's almost like she can't stand the sight of me."

Unfortunately, there are times when, no matter how assertive or creative you are, you won't be able to make a dent in your stepmother's armor. It's not your fault. Remember, it takes two to have a relationship. Talking it out with someone else might help. Sometimes, however, girls report that when they speak with their dads, they aren't sympathetic, or believe that their daughters are putting them in the middle. Then girls end up feeling even more upset, disappointed, or hurt. If this happens, it doesn't mean you've done anything wrong. It may be a good time to turn to a trusted relative, guidance counselor, religious leader, or family counselor.

COMPETITION WITH MOM

As if dealing with a stepmom isn't tricky enough, some girls have to grapple with Celebrity Deathmatch featuring "Mom vs. Stepmom." Competition can be subtle, such as one or both of them asking questions like "What did your stepmother make for dinner?" or "What did your mother get for your birthday?". For Donna, 10, the competition was obvious and fierce. "I can't stand it," she says. "My stepmother took me to get a haircut and it practically caused World War III. Mom got furious and said that was her department."

The fight factor between mom and stepmom can usually be boiled down to one thing—insecurity. Both of them are unsure of their positions in your life now, and each of them is probably just a tad jealous of the other.

The best policy: keep mom and stepmom apart. Don't talk about one to the other, and don't give either of them the bitty details of time spent with the other. If your stepmom makes the most delicious holiday cookies you've ever tasted, do not (we repeat, do not) get the recipe for your mom and suggest she give it a whirl.

Same goes for the other direction. If your mom asks you about your stepmom, you might think you should tell all—after all, she's your mom. But this isn't about loyalty. You never know when a teensy bit of info can cause a heap of trouble. So if either of them pries for specifics, tell them you're uncomfortable and suggest she ask your father.

WHEN YOU LIKE HER TOO MUCH

Despite all the pitfalls, many girls find themselves, to their amazement, growing fond of their stepmothers. So what's bad about that? Well, sometimes it can make girls feel disloyal to their moms. Bethany, 14, describes getting closer to her stepmother when she and her mom went through a rough bout together.

She says, "My mom and I were fighting so I spent more time with my dad and stepmom, and I found I could really talk to her."

It's not so surprising, really. Relationships with step-moms are sometimes less intense than those with moms. Over time, the relationship you have with your stepmom might evolve—less disciplinarian, more like an older sister or friend.

You may also come to appreciate your stepmother's finer points. She solves computer problems like a pro, makes the best tacos this side of Mexico, or proves a fantastic running partner. It's okay to like these things about your stepmother. You don't have to feel guilty or disloyal—it doesn't mean you love her more than Mom. There's always enough love to go around for everybody.

By being open-minded and positive, you and your stepmom can have a decent relationship. It might take time, but eventually you and she should find a balance that's comfortable for both of you. Stepmothers can be valuable people we both learn from and enjoy. And you just might find yourself writing your own stepmother fairy tale ... one with a happy ending.

The Girls' Life

Guide to Crushes

You're Not Sick, You're Not Crazy ... You're Crushed

Image 19.1

A new school year—you were just getting used to new teachers, mastering your ultra-stubborn locker and getting into the social swing of things. Then—wham!—you started coming down with some mighty strange symptoms. Your heart's been beating fiercely, you've actually started planning outfits and you're always on the lookout for someone—well, this one guy in particular. And when you finally see him, you find yourself blushing, stammering, and tripping over air pockets. Yep, you've got yourself a serious case of The Crush.

SAY WHAT?

Having your first crush can be as nerve-wracking as it is exciting. You're suddenly facing sweaty palms, obsessive thoughts and confusing decisions. Many girls wish their feelings would just up and vamoose so they could go back to their normal lives. Unfortunately, having a crush isn't something you can zap away.

Dana, 11, says having her first crush was like getting hit by a lightning bolt: "I could have used a little warning. I always swore I wouldn't be all gushy for a guy. Now here I am hoping I run into this one guy all the time." Many girls admit the plotting and planning can be exhausting. Every time you pass the phone, you will him to call. You find yourself lingering near his classes and trying to figure out his schedule. For Jenna, 12, scribbles were the big clue. "I looked down at my notebook," she confesses, "and had written David's name about a dozen times."

Sometimes having a crush is even, well, kind of embarrassing. As Jenna describes, "I promised my friends I would never put a guy first. But I want to be with David all the time. There's no way I can tell them that." Maybe you're having thoughts you vowed you'd never have: "The way he rakes his hair with his fingers is amazing," or "I can't believe how blue his eyes look when he wears that sweater." Now you're "one of those girls"—and wishing you could hibernate for life.

It used to be easy. If you thought about guys at all, it was that you'd like a cool guy some day, and he'd like you back. If only having a crush was that simple. Now in addition to figuring out your own thoughts, you're trying to figure out all of his. "What did he mean when he said 'hi' to me?" "Is he looking at me because he's interested or because he saw me looking at him?" "Would he think it was weird if I saved a seat for him?" It's confusing! So don't beat yourself up for having these feelings. Instead, give yourself time to sort through them.

BUT I FEEL LIKE AN IDIOT!

Your symptoms may not be fatal, but turning beet red every time you picture him is hardly comfortable. Annie, 13, reports, "Every time I try answering a question when he's around, nothing comes out. It's humiliating." Gabrielle, 14, confesses, "If he's in view, I can't seem to get from one place to another without tripping or dropping something."

If you've been feeling klutzy when you get within yards of your new crush, you're in good company. You're probably so preoccupied (being on the lookout for him and figuring out what to say) that you're forgetting other stuff—like holding onto your books or pushing the door open before walking through. Not to worry. This is all temporary, and you will function normally again.

OH NO, NOT HIM!

Just as you can't plan *when* you'll have a crush, you can't plan *who* it will be on. This guy may even be someone you'd normally put on your list of least desirable guys. It could be your best friend, the class clown, the super-brain who cries when he doesn't get an A+, or the guy who desperately needs a wardrobe consultant. Or maybe it's someone completely inaccessible, like your oldest brother's friend, your friend's older brother, or a Hollywood celeb with exceptional hair.

For Deb, 11, it was her piano teacher, who'd been giving her lessons for years. "It was weird. All of a sudden, I started playing like I had ten thumbs. I felt so awful, I wanted to quit." For Amanda, 14, it was the cashier at the local pizza hangout. "I constantly wanted to go there, but I didn't want my friends to know I had a crush on him so I'd always tell them to go without me." No one gets to pick a crush like a grocery item, so try not to feel disappointed about your choice. Life—and lunch—would be totally boring if everyone had a crush on the same guy!

CAN'T STOP THINKING ABOUT HIM

One of the most shocking things is how much your brain becomes consumed by "him." As Amy describes, "It's taking over my life! I've even figured out his schedule so I can pass by his locker at the exact moments he does. I can't take it!"

When you like someone, it's natural to want to see him. Problem is, you can't focus on anything else. Even when you have tons of homework, letters to write and chores to complete, you can't stop envisioning his milky-white teeth or the splash of freckles on his nose. You're constantly spacing out in class, reliving what he was doing when you saw him last. You're up all night thinking of him, even asking the Magic 8 Ball a million times if he likes you back. When it says, "My sources say no," you shake it furiously and ask again.

Mary, 14, claims the reason girls develop a one-track mind is the not-knowing part. "You like him but don't know how he feels about you," she says. "Does he like you back or hate you? You'll die if you don't know." It's maddening. So do you tell him? Not tell him? Flip a coin? Tell a friend of his friend's friend?

Let us make this perfectly clear: You don't have to do a thing. You do not *have* to declare your feelings. This crush is yours to tuck away in your mind and take out to savor. By keeping it secret, you never have to face potential ridicule, third-degrees questioning or humiliation. If, down the road, you change your mind, fine. Otherwise, mum's the word for as long as you want.

BUT I'VE GOT TO TELL SOMEONE!

Maybe you're dying to share the news. You're ready to blab every teensy detail to the first person who'll listen—the way he elbowed you, shared his world view, or asked if he could borrow a dollar (it was the way he asked).

This is a normal—but potentially hazardous—reaction. Once the info's out there circulating, you can never take it back. So tell your best and most trusted pal—exclude anyone who can't keep their lips zipped. If you're not sure you can rely on anyone, tell your diary, pen pal or secret-keeping cat. They'll never tease you, grill you or spill the beans.

If you're considering telling him—the dude of your dreams, that is—question your motives. What are you expecting to happen? At best, he'll tell you he has a crush on you too. Only what if he doesn't? Will you regret your confession? Also, consider whether telling him will make things too uncomfortable. If it's your best bud or math tutor, for example, things might get pretty hairy—and you do have to face this guy. If you know in your heart of hearts it can't work out, you're probably best off saying nothing. If there's as good a shot as any, it's your call.

"I'm doing it," some of you are thinking. "You only live once! Seize the day!" Okay, brave girls, if you're going to tell him, do it right. Avoid the bombshell. If you walk up to him and announce, "I have a crush on you," you'll put him on the spot. Even if he likes you back, he may feel too embarrassed to admit it.

STEER CLEAR OF MESSENGERS

It's tempting to hint to his best friend that you think so-and-so is cute. That way, you don't have to tell your crush to his face and put him on the spot. There's only one problem. You have no idea what the best friend is going to tell your crush. He might be jealous and say something mean, or choose not to tell your crush at all—and you'll never know.

If you have one of your people (a bud) talk to his people (his bud) you're really asking for trouble. Crystal, 14, can tell you all about it. "I asked my best friend to let his best friend know I liked him," she says. "Well, she told him during lunch, and the guy I liked started cracking up. I thought I was going to hurl."

So how should you let him know? Treat him like a friend you'd like to get to know better. Say "hi," save him a seat on the bus, share your notes when he's absent. Radiate a genuine smile. Basic skills apply: Start conversations, be a good listener, ask questions about stuff you're both interested in. Ask about a mountain biking trip he took, his old neighborhood. You get the idea.

DO NOT LOSE SIGHT OF THE WORLD AROUND YOU

It's easy to get so wrapped up in him that you abandon your old life. Some girls start skipping after-school activities so they can watch their crush play sports, perform in band practice, whatever. Lots of girls ditch friends to spend even more time around him.

Says 14-year-old Kirsten, "My friend Brittney keeps bailing on plans so she can drool over this guy KJ. It's so annoying!" Don't be one of those girls. Enjoy your crush, but don't take your buds for granted. If your grades or social life outside of him are starting to suffer, it's time to chill out.

YOU'VE HEARD IT BEFORE, BUT WE'LL SAY IT AGAIN: BE YOURSELF.

Maria, 13, knew the deal but still dyed her hair blond after discovering her crush's love for Cameron Diaz. "My hair looked terrible," she says, "and when he saw me, he started laughing with his friends." Others play dumb to get attention. Imagine hiding your smarts to impress someone! This makes no sense! If he needs you to be less so he can be more, forget him. The guys you want to hang out with should appreciate, not dislike, your know-how. If he hints he could use help surfing the net—and you know your stuff—show him the ropes. If you're a good athlete, invite him over for a game of hoops or whatever pick-up game you both like.

"HE LOVES ME, HE LOVES ME NOT..."

You can yank all the daisy petals in the world, but how can you tell if he *really* likes you back?

He's always cracking up when you're around. Guys get nervous too and are often more comfortable making jokes. If your crush always teases you (with a big smile), he may be hooked.

He's trying to be your bud. Is your guy being helpful, confiding in you, asking for help on an assignment? Is he showing up at your games? If you notice he's trying extra hard to be social, it's a good bet he's interested. Take note: Few guys are mature enough yet for this method.

He wants to know everything about you. When a guy gets incredibly curious about whether you'll be on the debate team, who you think is funniest on *Friends* and what your favorite flavor popsicle is, it's a good tip off he has feelings for you.

Dear Carol: I have a problem. I really like this boy who everyone else thinks is a dork. I think he likes me too, but he acts like he's afraid to say something. We're nearly best friends and he has the same interests as I do. What should I do?—BOY TROUBLE

Dear Boy Trouble: Who'll be going out with him? You or your friends? If you like him and he likes you, maybe you don't have a problem after all. And maybe your friends will soon see what you've seen in him all along.

Is he pulling strings behind the scenes? Some guys have a hard time being direct, so you just have to read between the lines. Does he pick you first to be on his sports team? Get you invited to a party? Push someone out of the way so he can stand behind you in the water fountain line? Definite signs.

THE VERDICT IS IN

You just found out he likes you. Now you're flipping out. Do you have to go on an actual date? Do you have to go public? No—again, you do not have to do anything. You can continue to be his friend, or not. You can call him on the phone, or not. If you're not ready to date, get together with him and other buds. Pace your relationship according to what you feel comfortable with.

Don't let friends or anyone else push you into anything. You can just enjoy the fact that he has feelings for you too. If, on the other hand, you learn he's not interested, it's his big loss. We know it feels horrible—that's why they call it a crush—but we promise you're going to be okay. It's intense, but it will pass. In fact, for good or bad, there's probably another crush waiting for you in the wings.

Remember to take things slowly and enjoy the good parts—like when you're so excited, you could skip through the school halls. The anticipation, the suspense, the bliss ... it's the best a crush has to offer. Live it up! Just remember not to let him become your whole world. And do beware of glass doors—you actually have to push them open before walking through.

Quiz:

Is He Crushworthy?

1. You and your crush are walking home from school together when you spot an injured bird. What does he most likely do?

   a) Wrap the bird up in his jacket, take it home, and nurse it back to health.

   b) Say, "Hmm, looks like a rare species from the Laguna tribe."

   c) Poke it with a stick and pluck a feather for his collection.

2. You ask your crush if he wants to go to the carnival with you, but he says he can't make it. When you spot him there with his friends he says:

   a) "I'm really sorry. I was planning on staying home to study for the history exam, but the guys talked me into going out instead."

   b) Nothing. As soon as he sees you, he bolts behind the cotton candy counter.

c) "Well, see, my aunt died and I was supposed to go to the funeral, but the thing got postponed 'til next Friday."

3. You tell your guy a funny story that happened at summer camp. How does he respond?

    a) Laughs and tells you how hilarious you are.

    b) Says, "Yeah, so? Guess what happened to Hunter at camp..."

    c) Yawns and says, "Huh? I don't get it."

4. You're at the mall with your boy, and you walk into Wacky Willy's Silly Sweets. What does your crush do?

    a) Buys you a bouquet of lollipops.

    b) Gets himself a jawbreaker and asks if you want a taste.

    c) Slips a handful of gummy worms into his pocket and leaves the store without paying.

5. You run into your crush at Skateland. His appearance is as follows:

Image 20.1

a) Khaki pants, a nice shirt and a new haircut. And, mmm, is that CK One you smell?

b) A pair of jeans and a T-shirt that looks like it was yanked from the dirty laundry pile.

c) A pair of cut-offs and a shirt that says, "Who Cut the Cheese?"

6. Your guy agrees to help you study after school for tomorrow's language arts test. How does he follow up?

a) Shows up on time, equipped with *Webster's, Roget's* and the newest edition of the *Prentice-Hall Handbook for Writers.*

b) Knocks on the door twenty minutes late with three of his friends by his side and says, "Can we make this quick? I have a basketball game in half an hour."

c) Stands you up entirely, doesn't call, and avoids you the next day.

7. You're walking with your guy when you trip and fall flat on your face. How does he react?

a) Helps you up, wipes gravel off your knees, and seems genuinely concerned.

b) Asks, "You all right?"

c) Keeps walking, shakes his head and mutters, "Klutz."

8. You're at the park and your crush is hangin' out with some of his friends. Suddenly, his mom yells for him, "Ed-waaaard!" How does he respond?

    a) "Must be time for dinner. Gotta go, guys."

    b) No response. He pretends he doesn't hear her, hangs out for about ten minutes longer and then moseys on home.

    c) "I have no idea why she insists on calling me Edward. Everyone knows I'm Big E." (Image 20.1)

9. You invite your favorite boy to your house for dinner so your parents can meet him. What is his conduct at the dinner table?

    a) He puts his napkin in his lap, holds his fork correctly, and says, "These are the best brussels sprouts I've ever tasted. How did you make them?"

    b) He cleans his plate but skips the dinner conversation.

    c) He dips his half-chewed roll in the gravy boat, licks his butter knife, and recaps last night's *South Park*—word for word.

10. An older kid in the school parking lot offers your guy a cigarette. He says:

a) "No thanks, man. I don't smoke."

b) "Well, maybe. I'll try anything once."

c) "Gotta light?"

11. Your school is devising a gender equity program so girls are sure to get fair treatment in education and sports. What does your guy do to participate?

a) Helps you write a letter of support to submit to the board of education.

b) Asks, "Gender what?"

c) Paints posters that read, "Hey, girls! Forget what's fair. Go do your hair!"

12. A big science project is due on Monday. What does your boy do to prepare?

a) Spends all weekend collecting data to support his hypothesis on water conservation.

b) Sticks the stem of a pinwheel inside a soda bottle and calls it a windmill.

c) Knocks over the smartest kid in class, steals his ant colony, and turns it in as his own.

SCORING

Mark 3 points for each A answer, 2 points for Bs, 1 for Cs. Add up the total.

28-36 points: Good for you. You know you deserve the best and won't settle for anything less. You have no interest in wasting your time on a guy who isn't caring and respectful of girls. Congrats on having a good eye, and have a blast with this sweetheart of a guy.

20-27 points: While your crush has potential, he's probably not quite ready for a girlfriend just yet. Spend time hanging out with him in group situations, which will give you a chance to check out whether he's worth your energy. Hey, he might come around and grow up some. But if he doesn't, you can still keep him around as a bud.

12-19 points: Turn around right now, and run (don't jog)—as fast as you can! This guy is trouble and certainly not worth your time. He's soooooo cute, you say? He's also rude, inconsiderate, and dishonest. Trust us—cute only goes so far when he lies to you for the ninth time in a row. Say goodbye to this crush, and work on setting your sights a little higher.

Controlling The "Crush Crazies"

It doesn't take a brain surgeon to figure out what a new crush can do to a girl. Suddenly, you smile a little bigger. Your step has an extra bounce. You think nothing of rolling out of bed at 5:45A.M. to blow your hair dry. Yes, now that your crush has come along, each new day brims with possibility. Even though it's November, you're sure you hear birds singing as you pass his locker. The rain outside isn't cold and dreary anymore; now it's cozy and romantic.

The buzz you get from having a new crush couldn't be matched by ten gallons of Frappuccino. But as good as having a crush can feel, it is our duty to inform you of one tiny detail—love can turn you loony.

Don't believe it? That's the funny thing about the crush crazies. They strike otherwise perfectly normal girls. Take Jen. At the peak of her crush, she would take her chocolate lab Java for his nightly walk around the block. Then she'd hike it an extra twenty—that's 20!—blocks north, on the off chance she might "bump into" her crush near his house.

Then there's Claire. Her crush gave her the number to his private line so they could discuss sets they were building for the school production of *South Pacific*. Two months later, Claire was still calling the number—just to hear his voice on his answering machine. Even though she worried that he might have had caller ID, "but since he never had me arrested," she just kept on calling.

Don't get us wrong. We're not talking about those little things you do to give fate the extra nudge it needs to bring you together with your crush. There's no harm in consulting your Magic 8-ball or passing by his locker on occasion. We're talking about the things we do for love that later cause us to do a V-8 headslap.

Each of us have probably had a few "What was I thinking?!?" moments that make us cringe in retrospect. But don't be so hard on yourself—after all, you weren't thinking. The crush crazies were thinking for you. The bad news is even the most sane, level-headed girl can find herself caving in to the crush crazies. The trick is to take a chance on romance—without turning into a fool for love. Below are some smart crush moves to make sure you're staying sane.

SMART CRUSH MOVE NO.1: BE SURE HE IS WORTHY

One of the weird things about the crush crazies is they tend to strike hardest when your crush is someone you only know from afar. Let's say you're a freshman and you fall like a rock for the captain of the football team, a senior. He's all you think about. It matters not that you have no classes with this guy and no mutual friends. Heck, you and he are barely on "hello" terms. But from where you sit in the bleachers, he has it all—he's great looking, an awesome athlete, someone who has a lot of pull with people in school. He's perfect—and you must have him. (Image 21.1)

Hate to be the one to burst your love bubble, but guess what? He's not perfect. You just haven't had the chance to find that out yet. Still, you are willing to stake your happiness on whether or not this is the week he figures out your name is Bridget, not Brittany.

It's disappointing when a crush doesn't reciprocate the same amount of attention and affection you dish out for him. But when you stop to think about it, how could he? While Joe Pigskin is off pumping iron three hours each night (you don't get those biceps by staying home with a good book), you've been day-dreaming about how awesome it would be to have him as a boyfriend. But what do you really know about him? Do you have common interests? Would he support your efforts to write your first novel by eighteen? Who knows? You don't.

Image 21.1

It's not that you shouldn't be flexible in your expectations or that you shouldn't consider someone who is your social or personal opposite. Some great romances happen between people who outwardly might not have much in common. But there has to be respect, caring, and understanding. Unless you have a sense of who your crush truly is, it's foolish to put all your happiness eggs in his basket. No matter how cute his basket is.

No doubt, it's fun to like someone from afar—and safe. You never have to risk rejection or find yourself in dating situations you may not feel ready for if your relationship is limited to writing his name on the bottom of your shoe. And it's perfectly okay to have a "schoolgirl" crush on people like celebrities and athletes as long as you recognize your admiration for what it is—a starry-eyed crush. (And if you are going to crush on a football player, may we recommend Brett Favre?)

But if you're ready to consider dating, look around your own group for guys you know and respect. Save your feelings for someone who will appreciate, and, hopefully, return them.

SMART CRUSH MOVE NO.2: DON'T GO CHANGING

Once you learn more about your crush (He plays tuba! He drinks Peach Snapple!), the crush crazies tempt you to show your crush how much you two have in common. That's how Michelle ended up spending a freezing cold Sunday chasing her amour through a frigid forest—on skis.

When Michelle heard her crush was looking for company on one of his ten-mile cross-country ski-a-thons, she professed her love for slip-sliding the day away. Of course, the closest thing to cross-country skiing Michelle had ever done was on her mom's Nordic Track. Out in the woods, it quickly became apparent Michelle wasn't cross-country savvy when she fell flat on her face the second she tried to push down the path. "It was painfully obvious I had lied," she remembers. "He was bummed, and I was totally embarrassed." Her crush left her in a hut with some hot chocolate and a magazine. "That was our first date—and our last," she says.

Rationally, we all know pretending to be someone we aren't is a bad idea. But when you are desperate to find a connection to the object of your affection, it's hard not to chirp up with "Me, too!" when he waxes poetic over ski wax. But before you find yourself hugging a pine instead of pining away, search for the truth in what is about to fly out of your mouth. There is nothing wrong with saying, "Wow, you can ski ten miles? I can't go ten feet, but I'd love to learn."

Why would that have been a smarter move? Because for most guys, the only thing better than mastering an activity is sharing that knowledge with someone else. Whether your crush writes cool song lyrics, plays piano, or is an awesome cook, one of the nicest things you can do for him is show a real interest in what he loves most. Who knows? He might get a clue and offer you a lesson. But if, after your best efforts, you can't stand the cold, then get out of the, um, forest.

SMART CRUSH MOVE NO.3: DON'T SHOW AND DON'T TELL

If you really want a "Thank heavens that wasn't me" moment, try Shari's story on for size. She had a huge crush on the star of the freshman lacrosse team. When the team reached the finals, she thought it would be fun to show her support by making a T-shirt with his picture and a big #1.

"I scanned in a photo I snapped at a game and transferred it to a T-shirt. I thought it would be a cool way to show him I care. Of course, his team-mates saw me wearing it and started laughing and teasing him. He was nice about it, but it was obvious I had blown it."

Dear Carol: One of my BFFs is starting to like boys and my other friends and I are not ready for that. She's always fixing her hair, while my friends and I don't care if our hair looks like it's been in a twister. When I have her over, all she talks about is boys, and if I had my way, I would ship boys off to Planet X! I have known her for six years so I don't really want to dump her.—CUPID IS STUPID

Dear Cupid Is Stupid: Then don't dump her. Your long-term friendship doesn't have to screech to a halt just because you're going through different phases or have different interests. Boy-crazy girls can be best friends with book-crazy girls or horse-crazy girls or artistic girls or athletic girls. Don't criticize your friend, but next time she's going on and on about the hottie in homeroom, say, "I know you like him, but now I want to talk about..." and come up with a common interest such as books or movies. Here's another idea—spend time together doing something besides yakking. Bake cupcakes, ride bicycles, visit a pet store, rent a movie, or study for the science test.

When you're crush crazy, it's easy to think a stunt like Shari's will be a welcome ice-breaker. But more often than not, big gestures fall flat. Why? First, most guys hate being put on the spot. When you go over the top to get noticed, you are, in a way, forcing your crush to make a decision he might not be ready for. You may have been working on this crush for months, but on his radar screen, you are barely a blip. Asking him to like you before he knows you is totally unfair.

CRUSH HORROR STORIES

If you're feeling heartbroken over your new crush, here are some girls who can truly sympathize. Despite their experiences, they all lived to tell the tale!

"Jimmy was an outdoor nut, so I told him I loved to hike—the biggest lie. When he asked me if I wanted to climb a mountain in Vermont, I said okay, thinking it would be romantic. What a joke! I hated every step and got so exhausted I never made it near the top. I was humiliated."—MAYA, 16

"I had a crush on the lead singer of a band, and I went to see him in concert. He was amazing. During one song, he smiled at me and I thought I'd pass out. Then, at the end of the concert, he said he wanted to dedicate a song to someone in the audience. I was praying! He dedicated it to 'Julie, his brightest moon.' It was devastating."—ANGELA, 18

"I was ten, and it was my stepsister Anne's wedding. This hot college guy sat next to me and I almost died! All these pretty older girls were around, and he sat next to me. I acted chill at first, but lost my mind around dessert. He went to mingle with guests, and I followed him around like a puppy. When he went to the bathroom, I even waited for him to come out. To top it all off, I thought I should commit my smooth moves to paper. I wrote my helpful stalking hints on the back of the wedding program, which my stepsister found the next day. In case they hadn't gotten a good enough laugh before, they did now. Ugh."—IS-ABELLE, 15

"When I was fourteen, the couple next door hired me to baby-sit. I thought the husband was gorgeous (he looked like Harrison Ford), and I got shy every time he spoke to me. But he was super nice, always asking me about school and stuff. One night, when they thought I'd left, I heard his wife say to him, 'Beth has the biggest crush on you! It's so adorable!' I cried all the way home."—BETH, 17

"In junior high, I went crazy over this boy in study hall. He was a jock, member of the debate team, and in drama club. He was also three years older than me, so I thought he was really mature. Every day, I would rush to study hall so I could see him for as long as possible. Well, one day he was sitting with some friends at the table beside mine, and I felt something fly into my hair. I turned around, and he and all his friends were shooting spitballs at me and cracking up. He turned out to be totally rude."—ALICIA, 19

Second, most guys would rather get to know you without the whole school being in on it. When you publicize your feelings in a bold way, you are forcing your crush to come clean about his feelings—something many guys have a tough time doing, no matter how into you they may be.

Third, some guys get scared off by girls who are willing to go to great lengths to get them to like them. When I talked to guys who had been subjected to outrageous attention-getters, their reactions were mostly negative. Some guys wondered how their admirees could like them so much when they barely knew them. Others felt strong displays of affection meant the girls wanted a relationship more serious than they felt ready for. The most callous guys questioned the sanity of any girl who would like them enough to embarrass herself in public.

We have one word for you: moderation. There is no reason not to offer to help with his French if you're a francophile and his French sounds like Pepe Le Pew. Giving him a supportive smile across the cafeteria when he drops his lunch tray in front of the sophomore class is just plain kind. And if he's the one organizing the soccer team bake sale, why not offer to whip up a batch of your famous choco-mint chip cookies?

The key to success? Wait until you're on friendly terms. When you do something to show you care instead of trying to make someone care about you, you are more likely to get the result you want. So give it time—then give it your all.

SMART CRUSH MOVE NO.4: STOP WITH THE HAIR SPRAY, ALREADY

Before, it took you ten minutes to shower and two seconds in the closet to face the day. Now that the crush crazies have struck, you spend ten minutes just deciding what shampoo to use. And forget the closet—nothing is cute enough for him!

A word from the wise—relax. While TV ads show girls with shimmering, golden hair getting the guy, in real life, guys barely notice if you brush your teeth. Ditto the new duds. One guy we asked actually liked the girl crushing on him, but lost interest when she pulled an image switcheroo. "She looked great in jeans and turtlenecks," recalls our Romeo, "but then it was all mini-skirts and platforms. It's like she turned into the Britney Spears of homeroom."

The best advice? Be the same girl he already says hi to every morning. While doing your own Cinderella transformation may seem like a sure way to get his attention, it'll still be you on the inside. And if that's not good enough for him, then he isn't good enough for you.

SMART CRUSH MOVE NO.5: NEXT!

A smart girl knows when to cut her losses. While the crush crazies may convince you to hope against hope, there are good real-life reasons to move on.

First of all, there is only so much obsessing you—and your friends—can take. If, after your best efforts, your intended shows no intentions toward you, you must realize you might be better off as friends. As much as you might want a relationship, it takes two to make a couple.

Here's a good test: Would you accept from a friend the same treatment your crush gives you? If your friend never called and dissed you when other people were around, would you still like her? The crush crazies blind us to behavior that would otherwise send us running.

While it takes time to get over your crush, the girls I know were happy they moved on (okay, maybe after a few tears). Most couldn't remember what they were thinking when they liked a guy who ended up being a jerk. And, as many girls found out, not being known around school as "the girl who likes so-and-so" opened up a world of possibilities.

To Date Or Not To Date?

That Is the Question

Whether you're allowed to date or not, the idea has probably crossed—and triple crossed—your mind. (Otherwise, this book wouldn't be pressed so close to your face.) Perhaps you've watched your older sister get ready for a big night out and imagined what it's like. Or you've been rehearsing what to say in case your older brother's cute friend asks you to the movies. Or maybe you feel light years from dating but still have questions you'd like cleared up for the future.

One of girls' biggest worries is how to be sure they're ready to date—even if they have their parents' permission. To figure out this dilemma, think about why you want to date in the first place. If it's for any of the reasons listed below, you may wanna hold off till you're good and ready.

MY FRIEND IS DATING...

One of the most horrifying experiences on the planet (barring alien abduction) is believing your best friend is about to abandon you for someone new. So girls sometimes freak when they discover their best friend is planning to date. Your first thoughts might be,

Image 22.1

"What am I going to do on weekends without her?" "Will she still make time for me?" or "We made a pact to start dating at the same exact time!" Even when girls are genuinely happy for their friends, many also feel resentful.

Jill, 14, can vouch for that. She and Tami, devoted friends since third grade, swore to each other they would begin dating at the same age. That way, they could double date. They agreed to wait until they were sixteen and even pinkie-swore. Only, Tami's feelings changed one day. More specifically, they changed when Tami decided Jake, the new guy at school, was simply too incredible to pass up.

When Jake finally asked Tami out and Tami accepted, Jill had conflicting feelings. She was psyched for Tami, but also confused. Tami broke her promise to wait. While Jill wanted to be supportive and encouraging—she knew that's what best friends did for each other—she felt completely phony every time she confirmed to Tami how great it was about Jake.

Well, the date went great, and Tami became obsessed with Jake—telling Jill every little move, gesture and facial expression that was just the "cutest" or "sweetest" thing. More and more, Jill's resentment grew, and she decided the only way to save the friendship would be to start dating too. That way, she wouldn't feel so abandoned. The two could talk about their guys and share the experience.

So Jill asked out Scott, a boy from class she knew liked her—thanks to grapevine gossip. He eagerly said yes, and the two planned to go out on Saturday night. The situation would have been perfect if it weren't for one simple thing: Jill wasn't emotionally ready to date. For three entire days, Jill felt sick to her stomach. As she put it, "All of a sudden, I was worrying how I was supposed to act, what I was supposed to say or not say, what to wear, what if he tried to kiss me. But I didn't want to leave him hanging since I was the one who asked him out. The whole idea of it was making me sicker and sicker." (Image 22.1)

Which is how Jill ended up getting out of the date. Saturday afternoon she called Scott at home, and told him she was throwing up and couldn't go. She put off explaining until Monday, which she said, "was awful and humiliating, and I wished I'd never asked him out."

Unfortunately, this type of situation happens a lot. One girl decides she wants to date, and her best friend suddenly feels she should start too. Sometimes, it's a result of feeling competitive ("Hey, she's not the only one who can date..."), but more often, it's because, like Jill, girls are willing to do almost anything to keep their friendships intact. But the truth is, you can't force yourself to be ready for dating just because your friend is. What you can do is come up with alternative plans to keep you from feeling abandoned—hang out with other friends, find a new hobby, sign up for a sport. Do not let your happiness hinge on how your friend's dating life is going.

I'D LOOK COOL...

Maybe no one in your grade is dating yet, and you think it'd be awesome to be first. You'd look sophisticated and everyone would ask questions because you were "in the know." Or, maybe you want to show up your older sis, who's always bragging about this date and that. Or, maybe you think guys at school would like you more if you started to date—they'd stop seeing you as a tomboy and treat you like the girl you are. Whatever the reason, you're dating to impress.

Debbi, 14, admits she started dating Chad last year because she craved attention. "I was new to the school, and the girls pretty much ignored me—they already had their friends. I wanted to shake things up so they would talk to me, or even talk about me. So I asked out Chad, this cute guy who was a year ahead of us. Well, suddenly, girls were coming up to me and asking all these questions: 'What's he like?' 'Did you really ask him out?' I went from being a zero to Miss Popular."

DATING Q & A

What's the real definition of a date? According to Webster's dictionary, a "date" is: "A social appointment with a member of the other gender." Ugh, sounds like a visit to the dentist. Forget Webster's—we'll define it ourselves. A date is when a girl and a guy hang out together so they can get to know each other better. No more, no less.

Does there have to be a kiss or something for it to be an actual date?

Nope. It's the time spent together that makes it a date, not whether or not there's a kiss during that time.

What is a normal age to start dating?

No such thing—every girl is different.

What if my parents won't let me date yet?

Then respect their wishes. They're trying to do what's best for you. The good news is that all the daughters who've been told they can't date until high school have lived to tell about it.

What's a good date to start out with?

Going out with a small group of guys and girls lets you get to know him without extra pressure. Conversation will flow easily, and you can see whether he's really the cat's meow.

When I start dating, is it okay to ask a guy out?

Sure. Girls no longer have to sit by the phone waiting for a call. (We can't believe they ever did.) Again, group dates make this a breeze: "Hey, a bunch of us are going to the movies this Saturday.

Want to go?" Or, if he mentions after class that he likes mountain biking and you do too, ask him if he wants to go to the park.

What if he says, "No," or worse yet, "You mean with YOU?"

Then he's a moron, so don't waste one more second of your time thinking about him. It takes guts to ask someone out, and a cool guy will respect you for asking—whether he wants to go out or not.

What other advice would you offer when it comes to dating?

Don't try to be the type of girl you think he'd be attracted to. If you two are going on a date, that means he already likes you—for who you are. Inevitably, girls who pretend to be someone else will have to admit that they lied (which looks pretty silly) or be bored to death when he pops in his *Star Trek: The Next Generation* videotape for the umpteenth time. It's not worth it. Besides, you're awesome—as is.

And then? "I realized I had to actually go out with Chad. I couldn't just ask him out and not do it, or I'd look like a liar. So we went to this party. I was so nervous. I kept thinking he was going to try to kiss me, and I didn't want him to. I just wanted everyone to think we were a couple." Debbi says she was so uptight that she practically ignored Chad all night. "Finally, he asked me what was up," she says. "I had to tell him that I just wanted to be friends, which confused him, and he got really mad. So he went off with his friends, and I looked and felt like a jerk."

Cara, 15, went out with Eric in hopes of changing her image as well. "I've always been a jock," she says, "and I grew up playing football with the guys on the block, so it's hard for them to see me as anything but a pal. I started flirting with Eric to show everyone I'm not a guy. When he asked me out, I said yes, but I really didn't like him in that way. I felt bad about pretending that I had different feelings for Eric, so I called him before the date and told him the whole truth. I can't say we're good friends now, but at least he forgave me and all the pressure's off."

It's not impressive to date a guy in hopes of looking like a hot-shot. Like Debbi and Cara, if you're not ready, you'll end up getting caught in your own lie. What's really impressive is trusting yourself enough to wait to date until you are ready, and knowing you don't need some guy to make you a cool person.

IT'D TICK OFF MY FOLKS...

"I wanted to start dating," says Betsy, 14, "because I knew it would flip out my parents." Along the same lines as skipping chores and blasting music, dating before you get the okay is a sure way to cause friction with the 'rents—exactly what some girls want.

"I was so tired of my parents telling me what to do," Betsy explains. "They're always in my face about picking up my room, doing my homework, baby-sitting my little sister. I have to be, like, this perfect little girl. So when John, a guy on my softball team, asked me out, I automatically said yes. It wasn't because I liked him that way. I mean, he was nice and all, but I really just wanted to bug my parents like they bug me. I wanted to do something they had no control over."

Big mistake. "They freaked out when I told them," she says. "They said there was no way they were letting me go out with a guy, and we got into this huge fight. I told them I'd date whomever and whenever I wanted to and they couldn't do anything about it." Except they could. Betsy's parents grounded her and told her she'd better respect their rules.

All girls get mad at their parents at some point. And you will definitely stir things up if you choose to date against their wishes. But nothing positive can come from this. You'll end up losing your parent's trust, hurting a guy who doesn't deserve to be used, and sticking yourself in a tricky situation. If you're angry at your folks, sit down and talk to them—don't use dating as a weapon.

HE ASKED ME...

Girls often find it painfully difficult to say no to guys who ask them out. They feel flustered and lost for words, and it seems there's no time to even think about what to say. The guy is nervous and waiting anxiously for an answer. What are you supposed to do? It's awkward. Sometimes it seems the easiest thing to do is say yes.

This happened to Jennifer, 13: "Adam was this guy in drama club who I knew liked me. He complimented me and stuff. Still, when he called to ask me out, I was shocked. I sat there, not saying a word, wanting to hang up." Instead, she told him she would go out with him. "I didn't want to hurt his feelings," she confesses. "I knew how hard it was for him to ask me, and it seemed rude to say no."

That night, Jennifer couldn't sleep. She knew she should have said she just wanted to be friends. Now, she'd have to explain why she said yes and tell him she didn't want to go out with him. Uck.

So what could Jennifer have done? First, you never have to give immediate answers. You have every right to say you aren't sure. Here's a way to do it: "I'm flattered that you asked, but I'll get back to you." If he's cool, he'll accept that without pushing. If not, you don't want to be with him anyway.

If you know right away the answer is no, that's okay too. You might worry about hurting him, but you have to respect your own feelings. In other words, you take care of you; let him take care of him. Is there a way to decline and not hurt his feelings? Not really. It hurts to be rejected. The kindest way to say it is plain and simple: "I really appreciate your asking me, but I'd rather stay friends." You're done. If he tries to convince you or make you feel bad, just repeat yourself.

SO WHAT IS A GOOD REASON TO DATE?

There is one, and only one, good reason to date. You like a certain guy, and you want to get to know him better by spending more time with him. When you're ready and you've gotten the nod from your parents, dating can be lots of fun. Yes, nervousness is part of the package, but a good date also brings excitement and happiness. So stay cool about the whole deal, take your time, and prepare to enjoy dating for all that it has to offer.

Waiting For Dating

Really ... It's Okay Not to Be Ready!

Nervous stomach, sweaty palms, swelling zits, and brain spasms. Well, future doctors of America, what's your diagnosis? Hint #1: It's neither flu nor the common cold. Hint #2: It's temporary. For those who guess first-date-o-phobia, we see a long white coat in your future wardrobe. Dating is fantastic fun when you're ready—and a big fat headache when you're not. Since you have years of dating in your future, why deal with the hassles now? Pre-teens and teens all over the country are saying No! to dating, and opting for co-ed group outings. It's called non-dating, and it allows girls to paint the town red, pressure-free.

THE JOYS OF NON-DATING

"What pressures?" you may wonder. Well, let's start with pressure #1: avoiding awkward silences. He says, "What do you think of the new history teacher?" You say, "She's pretty cool," and he nods in agreement. You struggle for something to add, as does he, and then comes a deafening silence. You cough, hiccup, yawn ... anything to keep your mouth moving, while silently praying for an inspiring joke to come to you. As the silence stretches out, you consider running straight into a lamp post. At least you'd have something to discuss en route to the hospital.

In the real world, gaps in conversation happen all the time—with friends, parents, your gerbils. You don't think twice about it. When it comes to dating, however, males and females alike have decided that a lull in conversation is dating death. You have no business going out if you can't sustain a conversation for four hours. As goofy as this may sound, first-daters stand behind this line of reasoning.

Non-dating means never having to spew nonsense just to keep a conversation alive. ("So, Rick, what's your very favorite kitchen utensil?") In a group of four to ten, someone's always yapping about something. In fact, try asking a group this size to be silent for thirty seconds ... not a chance. It works out perfectly.

If you're feeling bashful or have run out of things to say on a non-date, let others pick up the slack. You'll join in when you feel good and ready, and it's easy to play off other people's jokes and stories when you're ready to go verbal again.

NO MORE LOSER DATES

Non-dating also offers an escape from those who are really getting on your nerves. Say you think Josh from math class is adorable. For weeks, you've been glancing back and forth at each other, but haven't had the courage to actually converse. You're psyched when you hear he's going for pizza with the gang tomorrow.

When you see him at the restaurant, he gives you a huge smile and motions for you to sit next to him—a flying start! You strike up a conversation, and all is great—until Josh asks, "Hey, why don't magnets stick to sweaters and stuff?" Later, he asks how to spell your name. (It's Sue.) Josh has the IQ of a paper clip, and your attraction to him has plummeted from ten to zip in under five minutes.

If this were a date, you'd have to ride through some seriously lame chat. Sure, you could survive, but only after hours of explaining that you don't have to be a boxer to wear boxer shorts, and that the "g" in bologna is silent (always).

With non-dating, you have the easy out of bringing others into the conversation. It's the social equivalent of Monopoly's "Get Out of Jail Free" card. Give your buddy Jason a nudge and ask, "What do you think about Josh's theory?" If Jason is a real friend, he'll pick up your cue and enter the picture. (Image 23.1)

Image 23.1

Carrie, 14, has used this survival tactic many a time: "I went golfing with eight of my friends, and this guy I had a huge crush on ended up being such a conceited jerk. So, when we split into groups of four, I made sure I wasn't in his group. Thank heaven it wasn't just the two of us."

Adds Lana, 13, "I went on this date with a guy from school, and we had absolutely nothing to say to each other outside of the classroom. I kept wishing my best friend were with us. That girl is never at a loss for words." If they went out on a non-date, her best friend would have been there.

If you do like a particular guy in your bunch, non-dating makes the situation a breeze. In addition to easing any social pressures, non dating gives you a chance to see what he's like with his friends—as well as yours.

"I like this guy at school a lot," says Liz, "even more so after we went out with a group of kids. He wasn't just nice to me—he was sweet with all my friends too. And he didn't try to show off in front of his friends. It was cool."

"In a group, you can take your time getting to know the guy you like," adds Allison, 13. "It's not like when you go out on a date, and the next day at school everyone decides you're a couple—even if you don't want to be. It's more relaxed."

Or, you might learn the guy you like isn't as amazing as you thought. Says Julie, 14, "Michael, the boy I liked, treated my friends so badly the night we all went out. He kept making fun of them. I was so disappointed, but let me tell you—that was the end of Michael."

I'M NOT READY!

Lots of girls are simply not into dating yet. Ask Lisa, 14: "Many girls in my class have started dating, but I'm not ready. I'm too nervous when I'm alone with a guy."

Christa, 13, says, "I have enough to deal with without getting mixed up in dating. But I like hanging out with some of the boys in my class, so it's fun when a bunch of us goes out."

Jody, 14, is considering giving up dating for now: "I went on a date last month, and it just wasn't any fun. I kept blabbing like an idiot, and I ended up exhausted. I'm just not ready for the dating world yet."

Other girls who'd like nothing better than to start dating have gotten the red light from Mom and Pop. Many a dad has firmly stated, "No way, no how, not until you're eighteen." Instead of getting stuck home, non-dating gives everyone a chance to go out and have a good time.

IT'S NOT FOR EVERYONE

While the group scene works for many, there can be drawbacks. Dalia, 13, is shy in a group. "I feel like I just disappear when I'm with a crowd," she admits, "but when I'm with only one other person, I feel more free to talk about things, my opinions. I guess I'm scared about what a whole group of kids might think about me."

Angela, 14, talks about the biggest problem she has with going out as a group: "You can't spend too much time with any one person. If it's a girl you're hanging out with, the other girls tend to get jealous or think you're being snotty. If it's a guy, your friends or his might start to tease you. You kind of have to make sure everyone's being included all the time."

Yonhi, 15, also says non-dating can be sort of annoying: "You spend half the night trying to find someone who wandered away. Or you have to wait while John goes to the bathroom or Lisa calls her mom. Sometimes, I feel like there's this big leash holding us all together."

Whether you prefer hanging out with a fleet of friends or one bud, it's good to know your social options. We have nothing against dating. It can be fun and exciting—when you're good and ready. Until then, nothing in the world beats hanging out with a bunch of friends, kickin' back and letting the good times roll.

Where The Boys Are?

You Don't Have to Go the Extra Mile to Find 'Em

At some point in your life, you probably will go on a date. You know that because you've consulted the psychic hotline, every horoscope you could get your hands on and your friend's Magic 8 Ball. But "someday" and "future" are just not cutting it anymore. Maybe you've been endlessly scribbling someone special's name in your notebooks, he who has yet to acknowledge your presence. Or maybe all you really want is the chance to befriend a cool guy—joke around, hang out, learn a little about how guys think.

The problem is, as you very well know, all the wishing in the world won't get a guy knocking on your door. Even when you actually see the "him" you want to get to know, it's not as if you have any clue how to introduce yourself. Maybe you're not even lucky enough to see a "him" that catches your eye to begin with. It's all so frustrating! Boy-girl relationships must be governed by some secret code you have no means of cracking. Listen up. Getting to meet and know guys isn't a big mystery. All you need is the ability to get out of the house, smile, and say hi with a little enthusiasm. A healthy dose of common sense won't hurt either, and that's something you absolutely have.

While we can't predict the exact day you'll meet your dream guy or best male bud—it may not occur within the next ten days—we can assure you it absolutely will happen. And until it does, taking the steps below will leave you feeling awesome about your new take charge, adventurous and confident self. (Image 24.1)

Image 24.1

GO THE EXTRA INCH (NOT THE MILE)

Girls have been wishing to meet guys since the beginning of time. It's only their tactics that have varied. If you were a Victorian, for example, you'd probably swoon (i.e., faint) or daintily drop your handkerchief to get a guy's attention. Today, as you know, some girls go to other extremes: wearing revealing outfits (e.g., sweaters that look as if they were spray-painted on, skirts that barely cover their bikinis); applying layers of make-up; or developing fake mannerisms (high-pitched giggles) that seem to say, "Hey, look at me!" Other girls try to entice guys by doing foolish possibly harmful things such as getting more physical with a guy than they should.

We all know these acts will grab a guy's attention in a flash, but the wrong kind of attention. Instead of enjoying the fact that he has chosen to spend time with you because he genuinely likes and respects you, you will know he picked you because you seemed to offer the path of least resistance.

So without these easy options, what can you do? Are you supposed to just sit there, hoping, wishing or praying that you'll be lucky and meet a great guy? No way! You don't have to sit back and wait for some guy to show up.

If you haven't been like Joey from *Dawson Creek*, growing up best friends with the fabulous guy next door, you may need to give your good fortune a little nudge. What we're saying is: it's okay to be active and resourceful, to go the extra inch to make something happen. This is definitely different than going the extra mile, which interferes and wreaks havoc with your respect and dignity. As you read the suggestions that follow, note the difference between the extra inch and the extra mile.

BROADEN YOUR SOCIAL CIRCLE

Being creatures of habit, most girls hang out with the same group of kids all the time. You stick together because you like each other, you're used to being with each other and—well, because that's what you do. Samantha, 12, believes her group of four girls is pretty typical, "My friends and I sleep at one of our houses every Friday, if we can. It's fun and stuff, but we hardly ever get together with anyone else." If you're with the same group all the time, how can you possibly meet anyone new?

Expand your social group. You can do this in two ways. First, think of joining non-school buds you've met through friends, Scouts, sports or youth groups, but haven't gotten to know that well. Liz, 12, offers what worked for her: "I made plans with my friend Claudia from gymnastics one weekend, and we ended up going to the coolest party. I met a bunch of Claudia's friends from her school, and we really hit it off."

The second approach is to include "new blood" in your usual group. If you're getting to know someone from class who you think would be a great addition to the next movie or trek to the pizza place, ask your usual pals if they'd mind if he or she came along. Shelly, 14, reports, "I really liked this girl from my Spanish class, but I was afraid of what my friends would say if I asked her to my birthday party. I'm glad I did it, though, because she's invited me back and she has some really cool friends." The idea is, each new friend you make can introduce you to other people, some of whom may turn out to have good guy friend potential.

---

supersafe.com

Tips for On-line Safety

The Internet can be a great place to make new friends, guy friends included. Being anonymous can make it easier to open up and get to know people. But when friendships are anonymous, you need to be even more careful.

A person you never met approaches you and asks you where you live and where you go to school. No chance you'd ever reveal that information, right? Well, millions of girls do it every day. Almost all the people you chat with on-line are just fellow information superhighway travelers like yourself, but there is the possibility of someone pretending to be someone they're not.

Even kids with computer know-how can still be naïve when it comes to safety. As a result, they become targets for criminals. Through computer networking, criminals develop friendships with kids by playing games or having conversations with them. The criminal usually then tries to set up a face-to-face meeting, where he can lure a child into a dangerous place. No matter how safe or friendly the on-line world seems, there is always the potential for danger. Always take these precautions: (Image 24.2)

Image 24.2

• Never give out personal information—your real name, address, phone number, where you go to school. That's why people have code names.

> • If anyone leaves obnoxious or menacing messages, do not answer. Instead, report it to the police and notify the system operator for the network you use.
>
> • Do not ever, for any reason whatsoever, agree to meet with someone you have met through the system. If anyone you talk to on-line wants to meet you, tell your mom, dad or another adult—immediately.

Part of expanding new possibilities may also mean rethinking some of your old conclusions. Perhaps you mentally eliminated some potential male friends with verdicts like: "too immature," "makes stupid jokes," "geek," etc. But some of these labels may have worn off. Before you realize it, some guys grow up and lose annoying habits. Going the extra inch means taking a fresh look at the kid who prided himself on belching the alphabet in second grade before you permanently cross him off your list. But it's going the extra mile to ask him over if you're just using him to get closer to his hot best friend.

EXPLORE DIFFERENT INTERESTS

A good way to get to meet new people (and that includes guys) is through activities. If you and he are both doing something fun, you already know you have that activity in common. An added bonus is that you have an instant topic to talk about, so there's less chance of awkward silence. Don't think you have to take up exotic sports like hang-gliding, skiing or scuba diving, either. Any activity or school club you join will do the trick. Believe it or not, Brie, 11, met David, who is now her close friend, simply by walking her dog in the neighborhood. "My parents made me walk my new Lab puppy to the park and back, and while I was there, David came by with his dog. We started talking, and soon we were meeting there every day."

You have nothing to lose by trying a new hobby, sport, or organization. Even in the worst case scenario, if you don't meet lots of new guys, you're at least having fun. Volunteering your time to an environmental or service project, for example, is not only satisfying, but it exposes you to people who have the same interests and values. These activities are all going the extra inch. But pretending to be interested in something just to get near a certain guy or to impress someone is going the extra mile—and tends to backfire. Geri, 13, can only now laugh at what happened to her. "I joined this science club at school because of a guy I thought was cute. But they were doing an experiment with rats and I almost barfed. I was so embarrassed I never went back."

TAKE RISKS

Going the extra inch might encourage you to take risks that you would ordinarily shy away from. By this we mean the risk of a guy ignoring you, blowing you off, or giving you a weird look. We don't mean risking life or limb. When it comes to taking a chance on friendship, follow the old saying, "Nothing ventured, nothing gained."

For example, many girls are reluctant to start conversations with guys. "I always wonder what he'll think of me," admits Arielle, 13. "If I say anything, will he think I'm dorky or pushy?" So what does she do? "Nothing, usually. I pretend I don't see him or wait to see what he does." What happens, typically, is nothing, because guys can be just as hesitant to take the first step. They don't want to feel dumb or rejected either. You don't have to wait for a Sadie Hawkins dance to take that first step in making a friend.

If you find yourself, say, on line at the video store with a guy who looks interesting, be brave. Smile and say hi, just as you would if it were a girl in line that you wanted to meet. If he says hi back, you're on your way to a real conversation.

And if he doesn't, so what? Don't assume you did anything wrong. He might've been straining to remember if he'd already seen the movie and didn't hear you. Or, if he did hear you, he might have been too shy to respond. If he truly felt too superior to answer politely, then you wouldn't want him for a friend, anyway. In that case, his loss.

It's going the extra inch when you take risks, such as saving a seat in band for a guy you like, offering to explain a math lesson when he was absent, or loaning him a book for his term paper. *Doing* his term paper for him is going the extra mile. So is doing anything that puts you at risk for getting in trouble or harming yourself in any way.

USE AVAILABLE INFO

Many girls wonder if it's okay to use info to their advantage. Belinda, 14, knew that a bunch of guys from her school's swim team were working as lifeguards at a county beach. So when her friends invited her to go to the lake, she suggested they go to the county beach instead. Why not? If you're trying to meet more people, it makes sense to put yourself in situations that you know can help you.

This isn't the same, of course, as going places where you're not supposed to be. Erica, 12, recalls getting in trouble when she and friends pushed that limit. "We stayed after school for soccer practice, and afterward our coach told us to wait in the gym for our parents. But my friends and I sneaked over to the football field to watch these really cute guys practicing. Our parents couldn't find us and everybody freaked out."

It's going the extra inch if you happen to walk by a cute guy's locker after lunch, when you know he always gets his coat; that helps a conversation get going. But it's going the whole mile when following him around becomes your only hobby, causes you to drop your friends, or puts you in places that are unwise or off limits.

SHOW OFF YOUR TALENTS

Unfortunately, many girls take the exact opposite approach: they think they must hide their talents—instead of using them—to impress guys. "I read somewhere that guys don't like girls who show them up," reports Monica, 13. "So I figured I wouldn't dive off the pier this summer when guys were around. I'll just jump in or not go in the water at all."

Whether it's a guy or a girl, however, a true friend helps you to be the best you can be. A truly great guy will be impressed by your brain power when you ace a final, admire your streamlined back dive, and beg you to teach him your method of whistling.

Trish, 12, won the respect of one neighborhood guy the hard way. "They always made fun of me for being a tomboy," she says. "which hurt because I sort of like this kid, Greg. Last week when I was the goalie in a street hockey game, I made a great save and he said 'Good one!' Afterward he came over and asked me where I learned to play."

What better way to catch someone's eye than being the best you can be? Any guy who'd need you to be less so he can feel like more isn't worth the effort. Instead, use your strengths. If you've got a way with words, pass a clever note or send a witty e-mail message. If you're a good artist, draw him a cartoon of your pokey bus driver. It's going the extra inch to belt out a few bars of his favorite song to make a bus ride more pleasant, but going the whole mile if the driver has to tell you to pipe down so he doesn't hit a tree. Similarly, it's going the extra inch to roller blade past the basketball court where he's playing hoops, but you're going the whole mile if you do so while shrieking, giggling, or wearing a bikini top.

BE YOURSELF

If you have to turn yourself into a pretzel to attract a guy, why bother? Remember, you want him to like *you.* Many girls try to conform to what they think guys want in a girl.

Zena, 14, says, "I overheard some awesome boys talking about one of my friends. When they said Gwen was way too serious, I figured I'd be just the opposite. Whenever I saw them, I tried to act like everything was a big joke. I'd be laughing and stuff. But then I felt so stupid and fake. What was the point?"

Zena's right. The only way you and a boy can be true friends is if you're both honest. This applies not only to how you act, but also to how you look. Copying flashy mannerisms or makeup may attract temporary male attention, but won't help you make a good friendship. Sure, it's always a good idea to try to look and act your best so that you feel confident. That's going the extra inch. But going the entire mile is attempting to act or look like someone else—simply because you're trying to please a guy.

PRACTICE PATIENCE

Yeah, *right,* you're thinking. We know, it's not easy. If someone whispered to you that in five days or three weeks or four months you would meet a fabulous guy, you might take a deep breath and relax. But when you want something badly enough, the thought that you might NEVER get it, no matter how unrealistic, makes you totally anxious.

In the past, when you really wanted something, like to play a certain song on the guitar, you tried your hardest, perhaps practicing long hours, until you finally got it right. The problem is, when it comes to meeting a great guy, sometimes your cleverest schemes and greatest efforts don't pay off right away. Sometimes it takes time—more time than you'd like.

Realize there's only so much you can do. In fact, unlike mastering fractions or free throws, this might be one area where trying hard (and, especially, trying too hard) may be inadvisable. Girls can do foolish things if they feel frantic or desperate to get a guy.

But there's never any reason to feel pressured. Contrary to what many girls think, there's no race to see who can have the first boyfriend, no prizes awarded for the most male friends. There is surely no definitive timeline for any of these milestones. The most important thing you can do is be true to yourself, be the best friend you can be, and have faith that you'll meet a special guy when it's meant to happen.

In the meantime, you can apply these skills to situations other than guy-searching. Meeting different people, taking healthy risks, being informed and, using your assets are always awesome ideas. You may find yourself having new experiences, taking an active role in making opportunities happen, and developing your talents in ways you hadn't imagined. You will surely become a more well-rounded and interesting person, someone a guy would be lucky to befriend.

Boy Friend Or Boyfriend?

At the end of school last year, Jamie, 13, found herself in a situation that seemed straight out of a TV season finale. All of her friends had sworn they were blowing off freshman prom to go to the beach—that is, until one of them got asked to go. Before long, everyone was grabbing dates and shopping for dresses. Boyfriendless, Jamie was bummed that she was being left behind.

Also bumming was Jamie's best bud Sam. Now all his friends were going but, as Jamie reports, Sam didn't really have anybody he liked. The solution for both of them? Do what they had done a thousand times before when there was a party or concert—go together as friends.

"I heard that a lot of the couples were really friends going together," says Jamie, "so I thought it was a great idea." So did all of Jamie's friends. Soon she was joining them in dress shopping marathons and master planning sessions.

On the big day, Jamie went to her friend Colleen's house for a pre-prom party: "Collen's mom hired a stylist to do everyone's hair and makeup. It was really fun. Everybody wanted to look awesome for their crushes but they were a little freaked out, since none of us had ever been to anything like a prom. Everybody kept saying how lucky I was to be going with Sam—someone I know so well and have a lot of fun with. I thought it was cool, too."

Jamie got home just in time to slip into her new dress and greet Sam at the door. "My mom made Sam and me have our pictures taken. I was totally embarrassed, but Sam put his arm around me and joked around. We finally got out of my house and walked a couple blocks to where the limo was waiting in front of my friend's house. I'm not used to heels, and Sam kind of held me up for the first block. He's always been thoughtful, but he was being really sweet. I figured maybe he was just trying to play the part of a date."

"Dinner was a blast. When we finally got to prom, we just hung out and talked and danced to a couple fast songs. Then everyone decided to go look for their 'hearts.' This girl on the decorations committee had made hearts with each couple's name in glitter and made a rule that when you find your heart, you kiss your date. Everybody knew it was her desperate ploy to get her crush to kiss her, but all my friends went along with it."

"Sam and I were the last to find ours, and I grabbed it off the wall and threw it in my bag, hoping Sam hadn't seen. Then my best friend told Sam he had to kiss me! Although I wanted to kill her, I laughed and dragged Sam to the dance floor."

"At the end of the night, I was really tired and my feet were killing me after spending hours in heels. Sam asked the limo driver if he'd drop us off early and go back to the dance to get everyone else. I was so exhausted, I fell asleep during the ride. When we got to my house, Sam woke me up and I kind of was stumbling and half asleep. Sam laughed and threw his arm around my shoulder."

I know this sounds ridiculous but there I was, lolling along with him supporting me, my head against his shoulder. And something clicked. Right then, we got to the door and he started to say what a great time he had. What did I do? I started babbling. It was something along the lines of, "Me, too, yeah, it was fun, okay, bye!" And I slammed the door. What I felt like saying was, "This has been the best night of my life, I never realized how completely great you are. You're the nicest person I know, and I am totally falling for you."

Not too long after that, Sam went away to camp, leaving Jamie to spend her summer, well ... confused. How could it be, she wondered, that with one simple arm-around-the-shoulder, her feelings for Sam could change so suddenly? Did she really like him, or was her imagination running wild? Could it be that he liked her? Did she dare tell her friends her childhood buddy Sam was now her crush?

Telling Sam seemed out of the question, but if she didn't say something how would she ever really know if he liked her? What would happen if they did go out? Would it be like friends, only better? Would they still be able to talk on the phone, complain about teachers, work on the school paper, shoot hoops, and catch movies as always? Jamie didn't even want to think about what would happen if they tried dating and it didn't work. Losing Sam as a friend seemed worse than never finding out if Sam liked her back. With only a few weeks left until Sam's return, Jamie was still sorting it out: "Two months and you'd think I'd have reached some conclusion. But I'm still just as confused about Sam as I was standing at my door after prom that night."

Jamie isn't alone. While many girls say the idea of dating their best guy bud is just too gross to contemplate, just as many are surprised at how their feelings can change. Friendships between guys and girls are hardly uncommon, but what might be new to you is the possibility that the two of you could be more than friends. (Image 25.1)

Image 25.1

ARE THE TWO OF YOU REALLY "JUST FRIENDS"?

Ben, 14, is sure his girlfriend Gabby, also 14, believes they are two friends who decided to date. But if you got Ben alone, he'd admit to a slightly different version of their story: "When we got to high school last year, I noticed Gabby right away. She's into theater like I am, loves cool music, and has a great group of friends. I wanted to get to know her, but I liked her a little, too. I had never had a girlfriend before, so I basically decided to just hang out with her and maybe something would happen someday. I'm not exactly someone who would just walk up to a girl and expect her to fall head over heels—that's not me."

It took a year and half, but one day Gabby found herself thinking how much she liked Ben. She asked him to practice a scene for an audition. Not one to shy away from making the first move, Gabby picked a scene between two characters in love, then, "I just kind of improvised my own scene. In the play, the characters decide they are better off being apart. But I started saying how I could never be without him, and how much I like him. Ben got the hint!"

We certainly don't want to make it seem like guys only become friends with you as a stealth dating technique. But, in some cases, you may be the only person who thinks you were just pals to begin with.

Says Gabby's friend Rachel, "All of us teased Gabby about how much Ben liked her. She always denied it. But, c'mon, the guy spent hours with her learning lines, calling her house, and watching *Buffy* on the phone with her. He thought nothing of getting up at dawn to wait in line for Lilith Fair tickets. You just don't really expect all that from a guy you're just friends with."

What are some clues that indicate things are more than they seem? For one, if everyone but you thinks that your guy friend has other thoughts, don't be so quick to dismiss. They are on the outside of your friendship looking in and may able to see thing more clearly.

Second, think about your guy bud's actions. If he skips baseball with the guys so he can tutor you for a math quiz, always tapes *The Simpsons* when you're at soccer games, and buys you your favorite cookies at lunch, this is someone who is trying to make himself indispensable. Still, it could all be for the sake of friendship. You have to evaluate the relationship and decide if he is just being his same great self—or if he is trying to hint at how great life could be if you'd only wake up and give him a chance.

TAKING THE RISK

Are you willing to give up your friendship to have a boyfriend? Say you're not the clueless one here. Sure, any relationship needs to be based on the same qualities that make people great friends: common interests, mutual caring, fun times. But do you really need to complicate it with a crush? Have you thought through all the possible outcomes?

Carrie, 15, and Steve, 16, were friends for a year when she decided to push the issue of turning their friendship into romance. At first, Steve went along with it. Then, he decided he wanted to be just friends again. It took a lot of work on both their parts to repair the friendship and get things back to normal. Says Carrie, "I had this whole romantic vision of me and Steve, how we would be the perfect couple. But the second we started going out, I saw less of him than when we were friends! I called him like always, but the guy who before would always suggest fun post-study plans suddenly didn't know what he wanted to do or how to dial a phone. I was completely crushed and felt like everything had gotten screwed up."

Carrie's advice? "If you're thinking about dating your friend, think twice," she warns. "I wish I had. If you want to go for it, pay attention to how he treats his girlfriend now. The one time Steve had a girlfriend before, he never saw her or called her. They broke up after just a few weeks. Once I thought about it, I realized Steve had never really been comfortable with the girlfriend concept. I guess I thought that would magically change with me. It didn't."

Even worse is what happened to Lisa, 15: "When we hung out together with a group, Jack was Mr. Easy-going. Then, we started dating. Suddenly, every time I talked to another guy, I was 'flirting.' Jack suddenly became Mr. Possessive. I had to break up with him, and I felt awful because he was a great friend before he became a lousy boyfriend." The bottom line is: He may be comfortable with you as a friend, but having a girlfriend could turn him into a nervous wreck or worse.

It would be awesome if your guy suddenly realized the girl of his dreams is right in front of him, but you are taking a chance when you put your feelings out there. We all know the worst case scenario: You pour your heart out, and he bursts into laughter. Friend or not, only the biggest creep on the planet would do that. Still, the unfortunate reality is that not every guy you ever like will like you back. Not because you aren't cool enough, pretty enough or witty enough—just because, well, it could be one of a million reasons, most of which have zilch to do with you. And once the cat is out of the bag, it's awfully hard to put it back. (We've tried; cats don't like bags.)

MAKING THE SHIFT

So how do you go out on a limb without sawing it off? Slowly. Very slowly. While it may be tempting to confess all to your friends, be careful who you tell. For some reason, this kind of news seems to bring out the matchmaker in everyone—getting two friends together seems romantic. So even if you make someone double-swear not to tell, word will almost certainly get back. This might not be the worst thing. If word gets back that he likes you, too, then yippee, mission accomplished. If not, you can laugh the whole thing off as dumb chatter and die a small death.

Stakes too high? Then your only choice is to keep being the friend he already loves to hang with. Try doing what Ben did with Gabrielle. Make yourself just a little more indispensable, a little more his biggest fan. Leave enough space for him to breathe, and just wonder a little. Sooner or later, not knowing whether you like him just might bug him enough to make the move. If it doesn't, if he continues to end every marathon viewing of cheesy monster movies with a "see ya!" then you have your fairly painful answer. The good news is that either way, you still have the best part of him—the part that thinks you're a really awesome friend.

WHEN NOT TO THINK ABOUT DATING A FRIEND

One of you has just broken up with someone. Everyone needs a shoulder to cry on when things don't work out. But nothing is worse than leaping from one boyfriend to another before you have a chance to get over the break-up and sort out your true feelings. Dating a friend is not something you want to rush into.

He just got a girlfriend. You never liked him—until he liked her. Uh-oh. It absolutely stinks when your best guy friend suddenly forgets you exist the second Miss Thing comes into his life. Don't mistake feeling jealous for other feelings. And take heart—when she's yesterday's news, you'll still be the one he loves to hang with. If his dating her is an honest wake-up call, wait until they are way, way over before you even consider the two of you getting together.

You want a boyfriend—any boyfriend. It stinks to be the only person without someone. But dating someone you don't have real feelings for is being dishonest to them—and to you.

He's dating your friend. We'll spare you the lecture about loyalty and valuing a long friendship over a very temporary crush. Again, the reason you two got to know each other so well is what you two have in common—your friend. Even if they break up, we say pass. There are many fish in the pond. Time to throw in your own line.

He's the class Casanova. He's dated every girl in your grade whose name starts with the letters A through U. And your name is Vicki.

Quiz:

Cracking the Crush Code

What the heck is he thinking? Does he like me or are we just friends? Here are some questions to ask yourself to decode the mystery.

1. He waits for you after school so you can walk home together.

   a) That half mile walk gives him fifteen full minutes every day to get to know you better.

   b) He has no sense of direction and is still trying to learn the way home.

   c) He's mighty fearful of stray dogs and wants your protection.

2. He always tries to be your partner in science lab.

   a) He wants other kids to know there's a bit of chemistry between you.

   b) He just happens to like that section of the room.

c) He wants to steal your hypothesis on algae growth.

3. He asks one of your friends what you're like—or who you like.

a) He's really interested and is trying to send you a roundabout message.

b) He really likes your friend and just needs an excuse to talk to her.

c) He's planning to blackmail you.

4. He's nice to you when you're alone, but distant and cold when he's with friends.

a) He really likes you, but his friends tease him mercilessly about the crush.

b) He has multiple personality disorder.

c) He's two-faced and can't be trusted.

5. He calls you up for no particular reason.

a) He's been thinking about you and wants to chat.

b) He's just bored.

c) Wrong number.

6. He tells you about his passion for bug-collecting.

    a) He's trying to open up to you.

    b) He thinks your backyard harbors a rare cicada species.

    c) He loves the sound of his own voice.

7. He tells you he's having trouble with the math teacher and asks for your advice.

    a) He respects your opinion.

    b) He's been asking everybody for advice, including the mailman.

    c) He thinks you're the teacher's pet and can get him on her good side.

8. He tells your friends something you told him in confidence.

    a) He's testing the limits of your interest in him.

    b) He's showing off to your friends that he's close enough to you to know your secrets.

c) Secrets burn a hole in his pocket.

9. He promises to call you at 9P.M.—but he never does.

   a) He cut his hand and had to go to the emergency room. Bummer.

   b) He forgot.

   c) It's his bedtime.

10. You write him a great letter from camp, baring your soul—and he doesn't write back.

    a) He's been spending time at his grandmom's and hasn't gotten your letter.

    b) Your letter was a little overwhelming, and he needs some time to think about it.

    c) He gave you a fake address.

11. He teases you in front of your friends about your freckles.

    a) He thinks your freckles are adorable.

    b) He'll probably want to tickle you when you least expect it, too.

c) He's an insensitive creep.

12. You leave your coat in the schoolyard and he shows up at your house to give it back.

a) He is the kind of friend who will look out for you.

b) He's hoping you'll invite him in for a snack.

c) His mother made him do it.

13. He bought you a big, expensive present that you feel uncomfortable accepting.

a) He's sincere.

b) He's confused about how much you really like him.

c) His birthday is next week and he wants you to buy him the skateboard he has been eyeing.

14. He tells his friends you kissed him last week after the lacrosse game. But you didn't!

a) Wishful thinking.

b) He's offering you a chance to test your powers of spin control.

c) He's trying to ruin your reputation.

15. You have one little spat and he refuses to speak to you for days.

a) You've been underestimating how much he really likes you.

b) He can't stand to lose an argument to a superior being.

c) He actually thinks he won the argument.

16. You met at summer camp. He swore he'd never forget you. Now he's forgotten to respond to your phone message.

a) He was so amazed you called that he's trying to figure out how to respond.

b) He has decided he's not big on long-distance relationships.

c) He has amnesia.

17. He splashes you while he's in the swimming pool. You're wearing your killer new outfit.

a) He'll do anything to get your attention.

b) He'll do anything to get everybody else's attention.

c) He'll do anything, period.

18. He kindly offers to break the nose of the guy you're talking to at lunch.

a) He wants to be the guy you're talking to at lunch.

b) He thinks the guy could benefit from a little rhinoplasty.

c) He forgot his lunch and wants to steal the guy's sandwich.

19. He wants to make plans with you that extend far into the future—like after eighth grade.

a) He thinks he's going to like you for a long, long time.

b) He knows you're smart and hopes to keep you around so you can tutor him for the SAT.

c) He knows his family's moving next year.

20. He tells you he really likes you.

a. He really means it!

b. He's been reading the book *How to Win Friends and Influence People.*

c. He told your best friend the same thing yesterday.

SCORING

Image 26.1

Give yourself 3 points for each "a," 2 points for each "b" and 1 point for each "c". Add it up.

45-60 points: You're reading this guy like a book. You can probably get a part-time job as an emotional interpreter. You have a gift for getting to the real truth about what people are trying to express to you, no matter how clumsy or awkward they do it. This gift will serve you well throughout life. Learn to trust it, and keep developing it! (Image 26.1)

30-44 points: You're on the right track to getting at the real meaning of what he's saying and doing, but sometimes you get sidelined by the sheer idiocy of his actions. Try to ignore the methods he uses to get across what he wants to tell you, and remember the hidden message behind it all.

20-29 points: Girlfriend, he may as well be talking to his fishbowl for all the understanding he's getting from you right now. But, don't worry—you can still learn how to interpret his strange signs. For those braver girls, simply find a quiet time to talk to him, and ask him straight out why he's done the thing that puzzles you. You'll have better luck if you're both alone, so no one can overhear and make him feel embarrassed. If confronting him isn't your style, reading novels about relationships is also a great way to figure out what's going on inside his head. Also, talk to your friends, and compare notes.

Dance Fever

Problems & Solutions for Your Next Dance

Knocking knees, sweaty palms, butterflies bumping around your stomach ... final exams? Nope. First airplane ride? Worse. It's your first school dance. Fear not. It's not as nerve-wracking as you think. Here are some of girls' most common problems for first-dance jitters and some smoothly chore-ographed solutions. (Image 27.1)

Image 27.1

The problem: You arrive early, and there's hardly anyone there yet. You and your friends are feeling stupid and bored.

The solution: Remind each other that you have fun together whenever you hang out at other times. You never needed crowds before when it was just your group, and you've all danced together around your room a thousand times. Stop waiting for others to make the fun—get out there on the dance floor and make your own.

The problem: A slow song comes on, and everyone in your group has been asked to dance—everyone, that is, except for you. You are standing there, by yourself, feeling like an utter loser.

The solution: There's no reason to stand and watch the couples until the song is over. Go to the bathroom. Get some punch. Talk to someone else who's not dancing. Go outside for some air.

Make a phone call. The song won't last an eternity—two minutes maybe—and you'll have plenty of slow dances in your future. Hey, here's a thought: Why not scope out a guy who isn't dancing, and ask him to dance the next slow song. He may be eternally grateful!

The problem: You ask your crush to dance, and he says "No way." He walks away, leaving you utterly humiliated. All you want to do is crawl into a bathroom stall and never come out.

The solution: The guy's a jerk! Anyone who is so insensitive and rude doesn't deserve to dance with you. Feel good about yourself for having the guts to ask him. The humiliation you are suffering is entirely temporary. He, on the other hand, has to live with his obnoxious personality for the rest of his life.

The problem: A geeky guy asks you to dance. He's the last person on Earth you want to dance with, but you don't know how to get out of it.

The solution: You can always say, "I'm sitting this one out, but thank you." But we'd suggest bringing him into your group to dance for a song or two. It took a lot of guts for him to ask you to dance, and it's not going to kill you to accept. If after a song or two, he's sticking to you like flypaper, tell him, "That was fun. I'm going to go the restroom." Chances are your Trekkie isn't going to beam himself into the bathroom after you.

The problem: You're having a blast, but your BFF tells you she's ready to go home now. But the night is still young, and you want to stay.

The solution: This is a tricky one and definitely depends on the circumstances. Did something bad happen to her, like she just got dumped or tore her skirt? If so, pull her aside and talk to her. The friendship comes first, and she needs you. If she's just bored or cranky, that's another story. You can tell her you understand she needs to bolt, but you'd like to stay and catch a ride home with someone else. If that's not possible, try to compromise on a fair time she would be willing to stick it out, like a half-hour or so.

BILL & DAVE CLUE YOU IN ON:

What the Guys Are Really Thinking

Why do guys hate to talk on the phone?

Dave: Because we have e-mail to answer, silly. Actually, it is not the phone that scares us, it's this whole crazy system that you females have somehow finagled. We have to call you, we have to ask you out, we have to plan ... and then we have to pay! How did this come about? Did I miss a vote? Regardless of our cool act, most of us guys are shy and shaking in our Skechers around girls. Think about it—we sit there with the cordless in one hand and our scribbled crib notes in the other. After dialing all but the last digit of a girl's phone number exactly twenty-two times, the phone rings. The girl can take the call or not. She knows she's in control because, well, we did call her. And therefore, she can shoot down every one of our well-thought-out topics like an Imperial Navy TIE fighter. The only thing with greater pressure involves a No. 2 pencil.

Bill: As usual, Dave speaks for all men. I would like to add, though, the dreaded end-of-phone-call-sign-of-affection problem (i.e., "I like/love you, too") which is fully expected by the girl at the other end of the line but results in intense social pressure, scowls and various sound effects if a fellow guy hears it. The typical guy just says, "Me, too," and turns red.

Why do guys dump nice girls?

Dave: To go out with cheerleaders. Just kidding.

Bill: Sheesh, Dave, no way. I only dump nice girls to go out with supermodels. (Kidding, too.) Guys date girls for a million reasons, not all of them, um, nice. The guys who only go out with the "hot" girls (I call those guys losers, Dave prefers "lucky") are most likely insecure and not cool enough to look beyond the superficial stuff. Instead of dating girls who are kind, have made a lot of achievements and are fun to be with, many guys look for the flashiest girl, even if the odds of a successful relationship are pretty slim. But not all guys. There are definitely plenty of nice guys who would love to spend time with a great girl. Unfortunately, you'd probably dump them.

My boyfriend and I go out for a couple weeks, and then he breaks up. Two weeks later, I'm almost over him when he calls, says he misses me, and we get back together for another couple weeks. Then it starts all over again. How can I get him to make up his mind?

Bill: Actually, it sounds like maybe he *has* made up his mind. He wants to date you for two-week stretches and test the waters with someone else, then go back to you. Good deal for him, not so great for you. You have choices: Play the long-suffering woman standing by her man; test the waters with someone new while he's doing the same thing, and then get back together when you're both ready; or dump him and move on with your life. The last option may seem the obvious way to go, but it's not always easy to do. Just ask Hilary Clinton.

Dave: I'd never argue that men are not pigs. What I would argue is that we only take our swinelike behavior as far as women let us. As soon as some-

266

one who matters gets mad, we stop acting like the low-life species we are. If not, then perhaps we don't care as much about our mate as she'd like to think, and the superior sex should figure it out. Pronto.

Is Valentine's Day a good time to let your crush know you like him?

Dave: Two schools of thought here. If you're a girl who needs an excuse to ask a guy out, then trumped-up occasions like Valentine's and Sadie Hawkins dances serve a wonderfully convenient purpose. On the other hand, I'd rather have a girl confess her undying devotion to me on some random Thursday in March than on Valentine's Day. Just write me a mash note in the colors of my favorite NFL team, and I'm all yours.

Bill: Valentine's Day is a hugely high-pressure day for guys in relationships, but it's a total freebie when a guy's unattached. What girls don't realize is that Valentine's Day for a guy is like Christmas for a Jewish person. You know it exists, and you see a lot of hoopla going on, but it's not your holiday. Expectations for Valentine's Day come from girls, not guys. (Image 28.1)

Image 28.1

This guy always majorly flirted with me. Then when I asked him out, he said no. What's up with that?

Bill: Maybe he had temporary hearing loss. Or he's an identical twin, and you asked out the wrong one. But more likely, he has a touch of fear of success. After all, it's one thing to fantasize about having a romantic dinner with someone. It's another to see that big green splotch of pizza oregano on his teeth. You can ease his fear by creating a low-pressure event (like going to a school basketball game with a bunch of other friends) so he can see that the reality is even more fun than the fantasy.

Dave: I agree. It is a breeze to be the guy a girl wants to go out with in theory. It can be downright flattering. However, it is a much more difficult task to actually be a guy a girl wants to go out with in practice. That's partly the reason a smart guy always seeks to be in the company of girls, even if they are not dating. It makes him all the more attractive if it appears he's a person girls like to spend time with on a regular basis. Beware the dude sans friends who are girls.

Do guys like girls who will kiss them right away?

Bill: If you listen to guys talk to each other, you'd think they really, really like "fast" girls. But guys are like boxing promoters—they tend to inflate everything by a factor of ten. So they'll say they're looking for some quick physical affection, but most guys really want what everyone wants—to be cared for.

Dave: There's a lot to be said for spontaneity, rather than plotting out a grand smooching scheme. If you really like a guy and want to kiss him (and you think the feeling is mutual), there's nothing wrong with letting him know. Don't make the guy play a torturous game of "Should I or Shouldn't I?" If you've decided you want to kiss him, go ahead and do it. I've never heard any post-practice locker room conversations along the lines of, "I had to dump her. She kissed me."

How can I tell if he likes me or LIKES me?

Dave: Ask him. Try to be funny: "Do you have a girlfriend who could beat me up in a fair fight?" The bottom line is that it is best to find out. There's nothing worse than not knowing whether or not someone you like likes you.

Bill: Eventually, you'll probably learn to pick up the signs when a guy likes you. For example, if he shows up for a date with his little brother ("Do you mind if we go to his Scout meeting?"), he may not like you as much as you'd hoped. Brings flowers? He likes you. Brings a book to read? Likes you less. Gives you gifts? He likes you. Gives you his cell phone bill? He likes you less. You'll pick up on these things after a while.

Quiz:

Are You Star Struck?

Have you ever been star struck? I mean, have you ever had a crush on a movie star or famous celebrity? Do you go absolutely ga-ga over 'N SYNC, or drool over pictures of Nick Carter? There are different types of celebrity crushes, ranging from the "almost nonexistent" type, all the way to the "almost over the edge" type. To find out just how major or minor your crush is, clear your starry eyes long enough to take this quiz!

1. You're talking to your best friend on the telephone when you see your famous guy on a talk show. What do you do?

    a) Politely wrap up your conversation so that you can go to the tube and hear what words of wisdom your crush has to say.

    b) Continue your conversation, sneaking a peek at the screen every now and then.

    c) Hang up on your best friend, sprint to the TV and plant your lips to the screen.

2.   When you daydream about your crush, what type of dream is it?

a) That you actually get the chance to meet him in person and get his autograph.

b) You dream about how cute he is, but that thought leads you to that gorgeous guy in your algebra class.

c) You fantasize about the day he'll propose to you. You'll be married right away, live in his two million dollar mansion, and live happily ever after.

3.   While reading the *TV Guide* you come across an address where you can write to your star crush. How do you use that information?

a) Write a letter to him, stating that you are a fan and would like to request an autographed photo.

b) You're too busy to sit down and write fan mail to someone you'll probably never get an answer from anyway.

c) You write to your crush every week, pledging your undying love and you make sure to include your phone number, asking him to call on a weekday, after ten, so you'll be home to answer the phone.

4.	Your celebrity crush will be attending a Planet Hollywood grand opening two hours from where you live. What do you do?

	a) You get there an hour early, hoping to snap a photo of him and maybe get an autograph. You're there to have fun!

	b) Get real! Standing in a crowd of 10,000 screaming fans, just to catch a glimpse of someone isn't your idea of a good time.

	c) You arrive five hours early, wearing your best outfit, and wait for your true love to pick you out of the crowd as his escort.

5.	You get the news that your star crush is dating a famous model, Zoe. How do you feel?

	a) You're a little disappointed, but you want your celebrity hunk to be a happy hunk, so you wish him the best.

	b) You've seen Zoe in the magazines. She's really beautiful and they look like a great couple.

c) You are devastated! How could he do this to you? You find a picture of the famous model so that you can draw a mustache on her face. Then you go to the salon and get your hair done exactly like hers and ask your friends to call you Zoe.

SCORING

MOSTLY As: MODERATELY STAR STRUCK

You sometimes have your famous guy on your mind a bit too often, but you keep the reality of the situation in check. Occasional daydreaming about your crush is harmless, as long as it doesn't interfere with your other important activities. You see the big picture and seem to realize that there are thousands of fans out there, just like you. You don't let your crush come between you and your everyday life, so it seems as though you can have your cake and eat it, too. You can keep your crush, but don't get too starry-eyed!

MOSTLY Bs: YOUR STAR HASN'T STRUCK

You don't spend much time daydreaming about celebrities and fame. You're more into what's happening around you and have many outside interests. Sure you can't help but admire some of those Hollywood hunks, but you'd rather focus your energy on getting that cute guy in your class. Once in a while, writing a fan letter can be fun. You might try writing to your favorite actor sometime, just for the fun of it! You never know, you might get a reply!

MOSTLY Cs: STAR STRUCK TO INFINITY AND BEYOND

You've got it bad for your Hollywood Heartthrob. You know almost every detail about him. He's on your mind much of the time and you'd rather stay home and watch him on TV than go out with your friends. You must realize how many thousands of fans adore your crush, too. While you're waiting for the slim chance that you two might someday get together, you're letting your life pass you by. Your family, friends, and schoolwork must take precedence over him. Next time you have to choose between going out with friends or watching your crush on TV, try to compromise. Set your VCR to tape the program, go out with your friends, and save the videotape to watch on a rainy day. Why concentrate solely on a celebrity when that cute guy just winked at you from across the room?

He Likes You! He Likes You!

Now What?

HELP! THIS GUYS LIKES ME BUT I DON'T LIKE HIM!

So you just found out this guy you know likes you, and you don't share those feelings for him. Maybe you think he's a cool guy, but you'd just rather stay friends and keep things simple. Or, maybe the very idea of him makes you want to head for the hills ... screaming.

It doesn't make that huge of a difference. Either way, you need to acknowledge that it took guts for this guy to put his feelings out there. The last thing you should do is make him feel ashamed about telling you. How can you admit you don't like him without making him feel like a reject? You can't. He is going to feel disappointed and rejected no matter how you say it. But there are certainly softer ways than others to deliver the news. Your best bet is to put yourself in his shoes. What would you need to hear to cushion the blow?

Ted, 14, had this to say: "If you don't like a guy, you should tell him you'd rather be friends. We all know that it's code for 'I don't like you in *that way*,' but it's a lot nicer than telling a guy you don't care about him or you think he's a geek."

James, 14, adds, "Be honest. It stinks to hear that she's not interested, but it's much better than having her play mind games with you. Once a girl told me, 'I don't really want to go out now, but maybe next month.' So I waited and waited and asked her out the next month and she said no again. I wished she'd just said she wasn't into it the first time. You've got to be real with a guy."

Mickey, 15, confirms this. "Don't go on and on about it. He's going to feel like enough of a jerk without you going into detail about why he's not cool enough for you. If he wants to know why you're not interested, he'll ask. And don't try to force him to be friends with you after, either. He might feel too embarrassed."

We agree with these guys and suggest saying something like, "I'm flattered and I think you're a great person, but I'd be more comfortable being friends with you" or "I think you're a great guy, but I don't really have romantic feelings for you. I hope we can be friends."

If you have no interest in even being friends with this guy (as in, you've always thought he was a complete jerk), try "I know how hard it is to tell someone your feelings, but I'm just not interested in you that way." That's all you have to say. If he asks you why or badgers you or makes you feel bad, just say, "That's the way I feel." End of story. You don't have to apologize.

A note to all those who think it's kinder to lie than admit you're not interested. It's really not kinder—and it can backfire on you. For instance, if you tell him you're not allowed to go to the movies with guys, and then he sees you with some guy at the theater two weeks later, you're going to look—and feel—like a moron. Same deal if you tell him you'd rather go to the mall with your friends, and then he sees you with another guy. Better to follow the advice from the guys above and stick to the truth. You and he will both respect you a lot more.

IF YOU DO LIKE HIM BACK

So you have a huge crush on a certain someone and find your thoughts drifting back to him all the time. Now, overnight, you find out that he has romantic feelings of his own reserved for you. While the news is awesome (more than you dared hope for), you're wondering about all the expectations—yours, his, and all your friends. How are you supposed to start a normal chat or goof around with him when you both know that the other is thinking, "I know that you like me. Why don't you just say so?"

"It's not natural," Jessie, 14, says. "Like with Kevin and me, I knew he liked me, and I wanted him to know that I liked him too. But once I told him, I couldn't even look at him. It was like I didn't want him to have this power over me—knowing how I felt. I knew it would change everything, and it was so much easier when we were friends and I could just go up to him and joke around." (Image 30.1)

Image 30.1

For the record, don't think guys get off scot-free, either. Most guys are just as embarrassed, if not more so, when they find out how you feel. As ultra cool as they try to seem, you can bet they are just as nervous once the beans are spilled.

Alan, 14, had this to say: "Last year, this girl from class told me she liked me, and it was cool and all. I mean, she was cute. But once I let it be known that I liked her too, neither one of us knew what to say. We both just sat there blushing. I felt like an idiot."

This isn't to say that you shouldn't admit your feelings or respond to his because you don't want to face potential embarrassment. That awkward-ness is sometimes a necessary bummer many of us face initially, and it can even add to the excitement. If you guys have stuff in common and enjoyed hanging out before, the embarrassment part will probably fade.

Dear Carol: I like this boy and he likes me so we are about to start going out. The problem is that a lot of my friends like him and they might be mad if I go out with him. Should I go out with the boy I love or should I keep my friends?—LOVE OR FRIENDSHIP

Dear L. or F.: It's not an either/or. You can have a boyfriend and keep your friends—you just have to be sensitive about it. Here's what *not* to do: 1. Act stuckup and make everyone else jealous by boasting about him and "rubbing it in." 2. Dump your buds in order to spend all your hours with him. Here's what you should do: 1. Act the way you always do. 2. Continue making time for your friends and talking with them about what's on their minds. They may occasionally envy you (they're human), but they won't hate you.

But if we're talking about one or both of you being downright humiliated and afraid to speak to each other, you may have to rethink whether you're really ready to put your feelings out there.

Sometimes girls feel more than shy or awkward when they hear a guy likes him. They feel downright scared about what's to come. This usually happens when girls feel the feelings, but aren't ready to act upon them. They worry they will be expected to go on a date as soon as the guy knows they're interested, or kiss him at a party, or start talking on the phone every night of the week. It's enough to make a girl keep her lips sealed.

Says Sandra, 13, "When I found out Billy liked me, I was so psyched. I'd liked him all year, and I couldn't believe he felt the same way. But when Billy wanted to know if he could call me at home, I suddenly freaked out. I mean, what would we talk about? Was he going to expect me to be all gushy on the phone? That's just not me."

Jada, 14, says that after finding out a boy from class liked her, she felt terrified. "It's not that I didn't like him too, it's just that I'm not ready to deal with all that stuff yet. My friends want me to go on a date with him so they can hear all the gory details, but I don't even know if I really like him. I think my friends like him more than I do."

The most important thing to remember is that you don't have to do anything upon hearing the news he likes you. You don't have to talk on the phone, date him, or do anything else considered couple-like. You don't have to do a darn thing—and that's true even if you like him. It's not about trying to impress your friends or prove you can have a boyfriend. It's about figuring out what you're ready for, and then staying true to that.

Alyssa, 13, knows how easy it is to forget this. "I went out with this guy Brad because he was the cool guy in school and all my friends pushed me to do it. I should have just told him that I liked him but that I wasn't ready to date."

If this is the case, the best way to tell him is to be straightforward. One suggestion: "I really like you, but I'd rather just be good friends with you until I feel ready to date." You don't have to explain or clarify why you aren't ready, nor do you have to give him a time when you'll feel differently. (How are you supposed to know?) Granted, he may be a little hurt or disappointed, but that's his right. And understand that it's temporary.

As for what he'll do next, he will either wait for you until you are ready, or he won't. You can't control how he feels or acts, so why waste your time trying? Instead, concentrate on just being you and staying true to your self and your needs. You've got good instincts, and when you're ready to move from admitting your feelings to actual dating, you'll be the first person to know. If he is no longer available or interested when you are finally ready, then he's not the guy for you. Someone else will come along.

What if you find out that he likes you, and you decide that you are ready to spend time hanging out and getting to know him better? Then you must feel wonderful! You know to take things slow and go at your own pace. You know to keep checking in with yourself to make sure things still feel cool and right. And when other girls go to you for support and advice, you'll be able to share your experiences, both good and bad, with them.

39 WAYS TO GROSS OUT YOUR DATE

We feel it is our duty to come up with new and imaginative things to do on a date. As long as you never want to see him again, that is. (Image 31.1)

Image 31.1

1. Guard your plate with fork and knife and act like you'll stab anyone who reaches for it, including the waiter. 2. Collect salt shakers from all the tables in the restaurant, and balance them in a tower formation on your table. 3. Wipe your nose on your date's sleeve. Twice. 4. Make faces at other patrons, and then sneer at their reactions. 5. Repeat every third word you say. 6. Read a newspaper during the meal, ignoring your date. 7. Stare at your date's neck, and grind your teeth. Ask if he's a slayer. 8. Twitch spastically. If asked about it, pretend you don't know what he's talking about. 9. Every five minutes, circle your table with your arms outstretched while making

airplane sounds. 10. Order a bucket of lard. 11. Ask for crayons to color the placemat. This is especially fun in fancy places with linen tablecloths. 12. When ordering, inquire if the restaurant has any live food. 13. Without asking, eat off your date's plate. Eat more of his food than he does. 14. Drool. 15. Talk with your mouth full and spray crumbs. 16. Scarf down everything on your plate in thirty seconds. 17. Excuse yourself to use the restroom. Go to the hostess and ask for another table. Order another meal. When your date finally finds you, ask him, "What took you so long in the restroom?!" 18. Ask the people at the next table if you can taste their food. 19. Beg your date to tattoo your name on his bicep. 20. Order something nasty for your date. Act offended if he refuses to eat it. 21. Ask for a seat away from the windows where you have a good view of all exits and can keep your back to the wall. Act nervous. 22. Lick your plate. Offer to lick your date's. 23. Hum. Loudly. In monotone. 24. Fill your pockets with sugar packets, salt and pepper shakers, silverware, floral arrangements—anything that isn't bolted down. 25. Slide under the table. Take your plate with you. 26. Order a baked potato as a side dish. When the waiter brings your food, hide the potato, wait a few minutes and ask the waiter for the potato you never got. When the waiter returns, have the first one back up on the plate. Repeat later in the meal. 27. Throughout the meal, speak in pig

Latin. 28. Take a bathroom break. When you return to the table, throw a spare pair of underwear on one of the chairs. Say they need airing out. 29. Bring 20 or so candles with you. During the meal, arrange them in a circle around the table. Chant. 30. Order your food by colors and textures. Sculpt. 31. Insist the waiter cut your food into tiny pieces. 32. Accuse your date of espionage. 33. Don't use any verbs during the entire meal. 34. Break wind loudly. Add commentary. Bow. 35. Feed imaginary friends or dolls you brought with you. 36. Shoot hoops with shrimp into his water glass. 37. Every time your date opens his mouth, interrupt and start a new conversation. 38. Belch. Score it according to the Olympic standard. 39. After kissing him, explain you're doing a study on the spread of mononucleosis.

The Girls' Life

Guide to School

She's All That—Or Is She?

Popularity Myths Revealed

Every girl wants to be popular. How do we know? Because feeling you're liked is one thing all people—young and old, male and female—have in common. (Image 32.1)

Image 32.1

But why is it so important to some girls to be in the "most popular" clique? Why do girls tear themselves apart trying to climb the popularity ladder? In the big scheme of things, why does being popular matter so much?

Here's the trickiest question: Why does one group get to be on top? Why are they so great? Do they have some special thing the rest of us don't? In order to find out, we talked to "popular" girls and asked them what the deal is. What we found out is this: There are a lot of myths about being popular.

Myth #1—People like you more. Wrong. Popularity means you're well-known, not that people like you. And even if popular girls seem to have more friends, it doesn't mean they have lots of real friends. Since popularity is based on reputation, girls often spend more time knowing a lot of people a little, rather than having a few really good friends. Said one girl, "I don't know what would happen if I ever really needed one of my friends to stick up for me and take a stand against someone else in my clique. They mostly look out for themselves."

Myth #2—You get to have more fun. Oh yeah? Everybody thinks popular people go to the most fun parties, have the best time at the mall, hang out and share the best gossip. Wrong. Our group of popular girls report a much different reality. "I'm supposed to be funny, pretty, look nice and be in a good mood all the time," reports Justine, "I can't just not talk to anyone one day if I don't feel like it." Lindsey also didn't have very much fun. "When you hang out with the popular people, you hang out with the popular people. That's it. I wanted to hang out one day at the beach with this girl I used to be really good friends with before them, but my other friends freaked. It was them or else."

Myth #3—You need to have the best house and best stuff. Like that's so important. Sure the kid with the pool will be everybody's best friend in July, but loyalty is not part of the popularity game. The girl who lives in a small house with a mom who makes everybody feel special can be just as popular as a girl with a mansion. The bottom line? As one girl sniffed, "You can't buy your way in."

Myth #4—You can make yourself more popular. Uh-uh. The word from popular girls is, don't bet on it. Making friends with all sorts of people is a great idea and good fun, but trying to break into the popularity penthouse is a waste of time. Why? One popular girl couldn't even believe we had to ask. "If we let anybody hang out with us, that would ruin the whole point of being popular."

Myth #5—Popular girls are happy. This is the saddest myth of all. With a few exceptions, most girls we talked to are really insecure underneath. In order to stay popular, you have to leave some people out, making them feel they don't fit in. Defending your territory and making sure no one is taking your place in the clique is exhausting and warps your self-image. One girl we talked to actually wished she could move to another state and start over as a less popular girl. "Once you start," she said, "you just can't stop and go away quietly."

Myth #6—The same people will always be popular. They wish. Again, some people are just so likable, they can't help but always be buds with everyone. But for the most part, popular people are like bell-bottoms—as soon as enough people get sick of them, they end up on triple markdown. It's safe to say that today's seventh-grade queen could be tomorrow's eighth-grade loser.

Myth #7—Popularity will go away. You wish. There are few things in this world that you can't escape: death, taxes, and popularity. Realizing that popularity is stupid and vile does not change the fact that it exists. What you can change is how you look at it and how it affects you.

BEYOND POPULARITY TO TRULY COOL

Want to know who all the girls we talked to secretly admired and wanted to be more like? The truly cool girls. Call them "most popular for the '00s."

Who are the new truly cool? The girls who are self-confident. They don't suck up to popular girls because they know who their real friends are. Truly cool girls set their own styles—no copying. Cool girls follow their hearts.

It takes guts to rise above the status quo. Speaking to be heard and letting your actions, clothes and attitudes show your true self is a bold move. Do this for a few weeks and you might notice something. Not only will you be happier, a lot of other people might follow your lead and start dancing to their own drummer, too.

And you might find that you have become popular with the most important person of all—yourself.

Books For ALL Kinds of Readers

At ReadHowYouWant we understand that one size does not fit all types of readers. Our innovative, patent pending technology allows us to design new formats to make reading easier and more enjoyable for you. This helps improve your speed of reading and your comprehension. Our EasyRead printed books have been optimized to improve word recognition, ease eye tracking by adjusting word and line spacing as well as minimizing hyphenation. Our EasyRead SuperLarge editions have been developed to make reading easier and more accessible for vision-impaired readers. We offer Braille and DAISY formats of our books and all popular E-Book formats.

We are continually introducing new formats based upon research and reader preferences. Visit our web-site to see all of our formats and learn how you can Personalize our books for yourself or as gifts. Sign up to Become A RHYW Registered Reader.

www.readhowyouwant.com